Michigan Weather

Richard A. Keen

AMERICAN & WORLD GEOGRAPHIC PUBLISHING

DEDICATION

To Dave

Library of Congress Cataloging-in-Publication Data
Keen, Richard A.
     Michigan weather / Richard A. Keen.
          p.   cm.
     Includes bibliographical references and index.
     ISBN 1-56037-046-7 :
     1. Michigan--Climate.   I. Title.
QC984.M5K44 1993   93-28792
551.69774--dc20

Front cover, inset: TOM BUCHKOE PHOTO
Background: JERRY BIELICKI PHOTO

Back cover: GIJSBERT VAN FRANKENHUYZEN PHOTOS

Acknowledgments

With its lakes, islands, hills, and changeable weather, Michigan is a meteorological quilt. Fortunately, nearly every patch of the quilt has its expert, and the true joy of writing *Michigan Weather* was in visiting and talking with these people and organizations, and then patching the quilt together.

Foremost among these experts is Fred Nurnberger, State Climatologist at Michigan State University. If you like the facts, figures, and maps in this book, thank Fred—he's responsible for many of them. Professor Carl Ojala of Eastern Michigan University in Ypsilanti provided some wonderful insights into such varied topics as lightning, tornadoes, and climate change. For details of Michigan's local climates I turned to the National Weather Service offices across Michigan; and Dave Wegenmaker (Ann Arbor), Dave Guenther (Marquette), and John Wallis (Sault Ste. Marie) were especially informative. Dave Soleim, a ranger at Isle Royale National Park, provided data about the temperature and rainfall statistics that you'll see throughout the book.

Rich Puhr of Detroit contributed all sorts of fascinating information about tornadoes, and Fred Ostby, of the National Severe Storms Forecast Center in Kansas City, sent me gobs of data about Michigan's twisters. Tornadoes are not just statistics, however, and Jerry Henry at the Beecher High School near Flint helped provide the human side of the 1953 tornado that leveled the school.

The chapter about "The Eighth Sea" benefited greatly from information received from the Great Lakes Environmental Research Laboratory in Ann Arbor. The long record of Lake Michigan and Huron water levels was kindly supplied by Gail Monds, of the Detroit District, U.S. Army Corps of Engineers.

Michigan's libraries and historical societies are valuable resources open to all, and I'd like to thank the folks at the Library of Michigan and State Archives in Lansing, the Marquette County Historical Society, the Jesse Besser Museum in Alpena, and the Sault Ste. Marie Public Library.

Finally, I'd like to mention an Army buddy, David J. Falk of Sterling Heights, who was probably the first person to ever suggest that I write a book. Dave and I were drafted on the same day in early 1969, and for eight weeks of basic training we shared many hours in dusty barracks and musty tents, and we tossed grenades, did push-ups in the sand, and washed dishes (thousands of them!) together. I kept a diary of the whole thing, which Dave found amusing enough to suggest that I publish it. I never did, and probably never will, because I find other things (like weather) so much more fun to write about.

Anyway, after boot camp I was assigned to a meteorological unit and began a career I'll stick with for the rest of my days. Dave went to a combat outfit in Vietnam, and was killed in action in 1970. Even though this book is about Michigan's weather, and not boot camp, I'm sure he'd like it . So, Dave, this book's for you!

CONTENTS

MAPS, CHARTS AND GRAPHS

THE LAND BETWEEN THE LAKES

■■■■■■■■■■■■■■■■■■■■■■■■■■■■

There's something special about Ryan Island. It's certainly not the largest island in the world, but it is the largest in Siskiwit Lake. Siskiwit Lake, in turn, is the largest lake in Isle Royale, which is itself the largest island in Lake Superior. And Lake Superior is the largest freshwater lake in the world (by some measures).

This bit of geographical trivia illustrates some of the complications and contradictions that make up Michigan's climate and weather. Sitting deep in the heart of the North American continent, Michigan is an inland state, but it is surrounded by water. Altogether, the Great Lakes comprise the second-greatest inland sea on earth (after the salty Caspian Sea in Russia), and Michigan's 3,200 miles of coastline are more than that of any state except Alaska. There is so much water, in fact, that Michigan's shoreline has been called the country's "Third Coast," and the Great Lakes the world's "Eighth Sea"!

Great as they are, the Great Lakes aren't the only—or even the most important—factor shaping Michigan's weather. A glance at a globe shows the main reason for Michigan's fickle climate. The 45th parallel of latitude cuts across the northern tip of Michigan's Lower Peninsula (slicing the fingertips off the mitten, so to speak), passing a few miles south of Lenloand, Gaylord, and Alpena. Hence, Michigan lies midway between the North Pole and the equator, and over the course of a year (or even a week) Michiganders see the weather of both places! Swinging between arctic onslaughts in the winter, tropical heat in the summer, and plenty of simply pleasant weather in between, Michigan has one of the most changeable and invigorating climates in the world.

Of course, there's a lot more affecting Michigan's weather than just latitude. Rain forests along the Oregon coast, the dusty chill of Mongolia's Gobi Desert, and the temperate vineyards of France all share Michigan's latitude. But unlike Oregon and France, Michigan sits near the middle of the continent, with land extending hundreds and even thousands of miles in all directions. Free from the moderating influences of the world's oceans, Michiganders are accustomed to 90° summertime heat and subzero cold during the winter—extremes seldom seen in France or along Oregon's coast.

Mongolia is also near the middle of a continent. But Asia is a lot bigger than North America, and Mongolia lies farther from any oceans than does Michigan. Mongolia is surrounded on all sides by mile-high mountains, with the world's greatest mountains—the five-mile-high Himalayas—lying to the south. Peaks and ridges effectively block the flow of moisture-laden air that might otherwise stream in from the tropical seas to the south and east of Asia. So, Mongolia is a dry and dusty place. Michigan, on the other hand, has only the Appalachian and Ozark Mountains between it and the state's primary moisture source, the Gulf of Mexico. The ready supply of moisture-laden Gulf air provides Michigan with enough rain and snow to keep farms and orchards productive and lakes full.

In a way, it may seem strange that Michigan gets much rain or snow at all. Most of the earth between 30° and 60° north latitude (and south) lies in the zone of the "prevailing westerlies." This band includes all of Michigan and most of the rest the United States, the exceptions being the Florida peninsula, Hawaii, and parts of Alaska. In this zone fair- and foul-weather systems move from west to east in never-ending succession. To meteorologists, "westerly" winds blow *from* the west, but if this always happened, wet air from the Gulf of Mexico would never waft north to feed rain storms in Michigan. Air streaming off the Pacific Ocean is moist enough, but most of that moisture is lost to the Pacific Coast rainforests and the snowfields of the Rockies. By the time Pacific air gets east of the Rockies and over the Great Plains it is quite dry, and usually brings mild, sunny weather to Michigan rather than rain or snow.

Fortunately, the prevailing westerlies are the world's most fickle winds, and at any given time may blow from any direction, including straight up or down! The prevailing westerlies may be thought of as a broad stream of air that circles the globe at about the latitude of Michigan. During the summer this stream moves north into Canada, and in winter it shifts south to the middle of the United States. Embedded in this broad stream are smaller whirls and eddies, and the stream itself may—like the Mississippi River—meander into bends and bows thousands of miles long.

The broad flow of the prevailing westerlies looks quite impressive on global weather charts, but it is really the little whirls and eddies that do most of the work. These whirls are the low and high pressure systems, also known (respectively) as cyclones and anticyclones or, simply, "lows" and "highs," that bring alternating spells of stormy and fair weather. The word "cyclone" comes from the Greek *kyklos*, meaning "circle." The air in a cyclone blows in a circular pattern around the center. This circular motion, however, can be in either a clockwise or counterclockwise direction. By definition, the air in cyclones blows counterclockwise (as seen from above), while in "anticyclones" the flow is clockwise. (Directions are reversed in the southern hemisphere, with cyclones blowing clockwise and anticyclones counterclockwise—this has nothing to do with Michigan, of course, but you might be curious about it.) In terms of air pressure—that number you read on your barometer—cyclones are centers of low pressure, and anticyclones have high pressure (this is true in both hemispheres). Low pressure is essentially a partial vacuum, so air streams into cyclones from surrounding areas of higher pressure (anticyclones). Putting all these motions together, air spirals outward from the center of a high-pressure anticyclone, and spirals inward toward the center of a low-pressure cyclone.

Cyclones come in all sizes, from tiny whirlwinds called "dust devils" to enormous regions of low pressure covering half a continent. To many, "cyclone" means a tornado, and tornadoes are definitely small and intense cyclones. Residents of Australia and India think of cyclones as hurricanes. Meteorologists around the world, however, usually refer to cyclones as storm systems that are several hundred to a thousand miles across, storms that bring snows in the winter and all-day rains in the spring and summer.

Cyclones have several jobs to do. A major task of the world's atmosphere (along with giving us something to breathe) is to equalize the earth's temperature by shipping hot air to the poles and cold air back to the tropics. If weren't for this exchange, the uneven solar heating of the planet would bake the tropics until they literally boiled and chill the arctic until the air itself froze. Fortunately, because of the large temperature differences, air currents move, much like the currents that develop in a heated pot of water. In the tropics, the trade winds (the winds that sway Hawaiian and Caribbean palm trees) and equatorial thunderstorms move the warm and cool air around. In Michigan, along with most everywhere else between the tropics and the arctic, cyclones do the job; their counterclockwise rotation (in the northern

MAJOR STORM TRACKS OF NORTH AMERICA
Solid lines show the main storm tracks

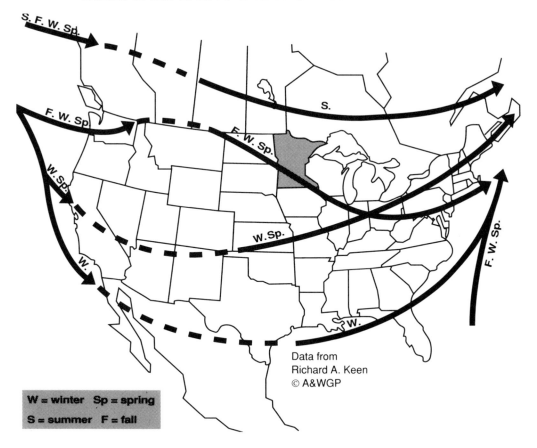

Data from
Richard A. Keen
© A&WGP

W = winter Sp = spring
S = summer F = fall

9

hemisphere) draws tropical air northward around the eastern side of the storm, and cold air southward on the west side.

As the swirling and mixing of warm and cold air within a cyclone equalizes the global climate, it also creates weather. Cyclones nearly always form along the boundary between arctic air to the north and subtropical air to the south. The importance of these boundaries was recognized by Norwegian meteorologists shortly after World War I. With the war fresh in their minds, they named the boundaries "fronts," and to this day fronts are depicted on weather maps in a nearly identical manner to battle fronts drawn on a map of the Somme River in 1916. Indeed, fronts are battle zones, with the clashing air masses creating turmoil far greater than any that humans can lay claim to.

There are four basic kinds of fronts. Before a cyclone develops, the boundary between opposing air masses may lie still for a while. These "stationary fronts" are usually fairly tranquil places with slow-moving patches of light rain or snow resulting in protracted spells of drizzly weather. But, if the air on the warm side of the front is exceptionally moist, heavy, slow-moving thunderstorms may result, unleashing torrential rains and flash floods.

As the cyclone starts spinning, the stationary front starts moving. A "warm front" marks the leading edge of northbound warm air, while arctic air plunges south behind a "cold front." Warm and cold fronts are *not* tranquil places; of the two, cold fronts are usually more exciting. Being heavier, the cold air shoves like a wedge beneath the warm, and usually moist, air. Forced upward, the warm air expands and cools, and its load of water vapor condenses into a cloud of tiny water droplets or ice crystals. Ultimately, these drops and crystals grow into rain and snow. Ahead of cold fronts the forced uplift may be great enough to produce thunderstorms and, sometimes, tornadoes. Along warm fronts the warm air overruns the cold air to its north, its rising motion normally gentler than that along a cold front. This shift produces more moderate but longer-lasting rain- and snowfalls. Although not as intense as cold-front storms, total precipitation during the passage of a warm front may be greater (many of Michigan's biggest snowstorms result from warm fronts).

The final member of this menagerie of fronts is the "occluded front," whose name comes from the Latin for (roughly) "shut out" or "cut off." After a cyclone has been spinning around for a day or two, the usually faster-moving cold front starts catching up to the warm front. Both fronts move like spokes around the low pressure center, and the "warm sector," the wedge of warm air caught between the cold and warm fronts, shrinks as the cyclone develops. Eventually the fronts merge, completely lifting the warm sector off the ground. With the warm air "cut off" from the ground, the fronts join as an occluded front, an indistinct boundary between two similarly cold air masses. Several thousand feet up, however, warm air is still being shoved around by cold air, and rain and snow are still being made.

Every year 30 or 40 cyclones pass directly over Michigan, and as many more brush by close enough to drop rain or snow on some part of the state. That comes out to one or two a week, which means that approximately every five days Michigan's weather does a complete swing from clear to rain (or snow) and back to clear, and from cold to warm to cold again. It's not an even cycle, however. Weeks may pass, especially during the summer and early fall, without a significant cyclone affecting Michigan's weather. At these times a huge high-pressure system over the western Atlantic Ocean, the famous Bermuda High of summer, expands north and west, and Michigan sweats in persistent heat. If the air is humid enough scattered thunderstorms may provide local relief, and occasionally weak cold fronts may skim northern Michigan, although most of the cyclones pass by well to the north.

From September through June, cyclones are a way of life in Michigan. October and April rains, December and January blizzards, and May and June tornadoes all mark the passage of cyclones across Michigan. Actually, several main storm tracks cross North America, varying from season to season. The Gulf and Atlantic coastal storm tracks are usually too far south and east to concern Michiganders, although occasional strays may find their way to the Wolverine State. Most of Michigan's cyclones have one of two distinct origins: the "Colorado Lows" that form over the southern Rockies and track northeast, and the "Alberta clippers" that drive southeast from their origins over the Canadian Rockies. The most frequent of these—the Alberta clippers—bring light rain or snow followed by an arctic blast, while the Colorado lows carry moist air from the Gulf of Mexico and may become heavy snowstorms. Summer lows tracking across southern Canada often barely brush Michigan. Not all lows follow these tracks, mind you, but they give an idea of where most storms come from and where they go. Keep in mind that cyclones may buck the prevailing westerlies and move out of the south or east; some of Michigan's worst storms have wandered in bizarre curlicue paths or just simply stalled over the state. It is this infinite variety of storms that makes Michigan's weather what it is: fickle, sometimes frightening, sometimes delightful, and always fascinating.

LAKE EFFECTS

Now we know why Michigan doesn't have the climate of Brazil or Greenland, or of Oregon or France. But the truly unique thing about Michigan is its lakes—11,000 of them that make Michigan's weather different from that of Iowa or New Hampshire. Of all those lakes, the four Great Lakes that surround the Great Lake State have the greatest effect. Two very obvious properties of the Great Lakes make them so important—they are big and they are wet. Their wetness makes them a ready supply of moisture to feed Michigan's rains and snowstorms. Their enormous volume means the lakes warm slowly in the spring and cool slowly in the fall, and help delay the progress of the seasons.

On a bright day in May or a blustery November evening, it may seem that everything within thousands of miles joins in the progress of the seasons. Right below your feet, however, there's a place where there are no seasons! No, I'm not talking about you-know-where, but about the clay and the rocks just 30 feet down. Heat moves very slowly in soil— only about one or two inches per day—and by the time summer's warmth has reached depths of 20' or 30', it's already winter again up above. As a result, 30 feet down the temperature varies by only one degree over the course of a year, and July is the coldest month! That's why caves and well water maintain uniform temperatures year round. So, most of the seasonal heating and cooling of the earth is confined to the top ten feet or so of soil and the air above it. What this means to Michigan's climate is that the sun isn't wasting its energy heating billions of tons of rock and concentrates instead on making summer 40 or 50 degrees warmer than winter.

Lakes and oceans are a different matter. As soon as the sun heats the surface, waves and currents mix the warm surface water with cooler water a hundred or more feet down. Likewise, as surface water cools in the autumn it quickly sinks and mixes with deeper water. Over the course of a year, all of shallow Lake Erie and all but the deepest waters of Lakes Superior, Michigan, and Huron sense the warmth of summer and the chill of winter. That's an enormous amount of water to heat in the spring and cool in the fall. As a result, the lakes' surface temperatures change only 25 or 30 degrees from summer to winter. Summer and winter also come later to the lakes, and the warmest and coldest months of the year are August and March, a month or two later than the warmest and coldest months on land.

The bottom line to all this is that on average, from October to March the lakes are warmer than the land, while the land is warmer from April to August. From May through July and into August, the lakes temper the heat of all of Michigan and especially the near-shore areas. The tempering effect is greatest when it's needed the most—during heat waves when 90° to 100° air overruns the state. The lakes, which may be 40 degrees cooler, chill the lowest 1,000 feet or so of this hot air, condensing it and creating little high pressure systems over each of the Great Lakes. As afternoon arrives, these little "highs" expand, pushing their miniature cold fronts inland, the welcome "lake breezes" of late spring and summer.

Like snowflakes, no two lake breezes are exactly alike, but the National Weather Service office in Detroit has compiled some interesting averages. The typical lake breeze starts around 1 P.M. and pushes one or two miles inland. On sunny, hot days with otherwise light winds, a strong lake breeze may push 5 to 15 miles inland, reach speeds of 15 to 20 m.p.h. along the shore, and lower the temperature at least 10 to 15 degrees within minutes. The strongest lake breezes occur in late May, when the temperature difference between land and lake is greatest. Right along the coast, the cool air cuts down on afternoon clouds and thunderstorms, sometimes bringing fog; inland, the cold front at the leading edge of the breeze can sometimes generate a thunderstorm or two and, once in a while, even a tornado!

In autumn and winter, when the land and the air above it are colder than the lakes, the local weather patterns are quite different. Arctic air pouring south from Canada can easily be 40° or 50° colder than the lake. For the air crossing a lake, it is like crossing a boiling pot; the lowest layer of air is heated, and hence rises. More important, the lakes deliver large amounts of water vapor into the atmosphere. On cold days you can actually see moisture entering the air as twirling streamers of mist above the lake surface. (This is called "steam fog." Take a cup of hot coffee outside on a winter day and you'll see this in miniature.) The lake heats and moistens the lowest layers of air at first, but as the arctic air passes across the lake, the warm, humid layer grows deeper and deeper. By the middle of the lake the warmed layer is deep enough for clouds to form, and the clouds grow into snow squalls by the time the air reaches the far shore. The squalls dump most of their snow within ten or 20 miles of shore, but the dissipating clouds can drop lighter snows and flurries as they drift across Michigan. Sometimes the squalls are accompanied by thunder and lightning, and snowfall rates of 5" to

10" an hour have been measured—the winter equivalent of a heavy summer thunderstorm. Lake-effect squalls can also bring small hail, sleet, and an occasional waterspout.

Lake-effect snowstorms become lighter and less frequent as the winter wears on, with the lakes steadily cooling off and starting to freeze over. The heaviest lake effect storms are in November and December, and during extremely cold arctic outbreaks in January. By March, the cold, half-frozen lakes have little effect on the air above them.

How important are the Great Lakes to Michigan's climate? A question like that begs for some numbers, so here goes. Statewide, Michigan averages about 70" of snow per year. Roughly a third of that—more near the lakes, less inland—falls from lake-effect snow squalls. Melted down, the annual dose of lake-effect snows amounts to about 3" of liquid water covering the state. That's one-tenth of the statewide average annual precipitation of 31". So, if we measure climate by the amount of stuff that falls from the sky, Michigan's climate is 10 percent lake effect and 90 percent other effects. But it's that ten percent that gives Michigan's climate its distinct character!

A TALE OF TWO CITIES

Muskegon and Madison (Wisconsin) lie 160 miles apart on opposite sides of Lake Michigan. Being at the same latitude, their climates would be very similar were it not for the lake. But the lake *is* there. The following comparison of various measures of the two cities' climates illustrates just how much effect Lake Michigan has. Keep in mind that with the usual west-to-east movement of storms and air across the lakes, Madison shows what the climate is like before the lake effect takes hold, and Muskegon shows what happens to the atmosphere after crossing 85 miles of water. To make the comparison "legal," most of these averages are for the same 48-year period.

SUMMER (July)

	MADISON	MUSKEGON	MUSKEGON IS...
Average daily high temperature	83	80	cooler
Average daily low temperature	58	60	slightly warmer
Average rainfall	3.75	2.42	drier
Average sunshine (percent)	68	73	sunnier
Number of clear days	9	11	clearer
Average cloudiness (percent)	56	49	less cloudy

WINTER (January)

	MADISON	MUSKEGON	MUSKEGON IS...
Average daily high temperature	24	29	warmer
Average daily low temperature	7	17	much warmer
Average snowfall (inches)	9.7	32.6	much snowier
Average sunshine (percent)	48	25	less sunny
Number of clear days	8	2	less clear
Average cloudiness (percent)	67	89	much cloudier

YEAR (all months)

	MADISON	MUSKEGON	MUSKEGON IS...
All-time hottest	104	99	cooler
All-time coldest	-37	-15	much warmer
Average temperature	45	47	slightly warmer
Average precipitation	30.84	31.50	about the same
Average snowfall	42.3	97.1	snowier
Average cloudiness (percent)	64	68	slightly cloudier

The numbers speak for themselves, but overall the lake makes Muskegon's summers cooler, sunnier, and drier, and the winters warmer, cloudier, and snowier. Taking the year as a whole, the summer and winter lake effects average out, giving Madison and Muskegon very similar annual average temperature, precipitation (rain and melted snow), and cloudiness.

HOT & COLD

■■■■■■■■■■■■■■■■■■■■■■■■■■■■

FIVE MILLION TEMPERATURES

If you took all the temperature readings made in Michigan since 1895 and threw them in a blender to cook up a grand average, you'd come up with 44.4°. This average doesn't include *every* temperature reading, just some 5 million daily temperatures taken at over a hundred weather stations across the state over nearly a century. At 44.4° Michigan ranks as the 11th coldest of the 50 United States—right behind New Hampshire and Idaho and just ahead of Colorado and South Dakota. But eleventh place doesn't really impress too many people. Without looking it up, who knows who our 11th president was, or who was the 11th man to step on the moon? So, let's pick out a few of the more interesting of those 5 million temperatures.

HOT AND COLD SPOTS

One thing that the 44.4° average conceals is the range of climates found in the state of Michigan. Millions of air conditioners help residents of southern Michigan get through the summer, while in the Upper Peninsula (U.P.) most folks rely on the lakes to do the cooling. And while peaches and tomatoes grow to a ripe old age in parts of the south, you'd be hard pressed to raise a carrot in some northern locations. Measured by annual average temperature, Van Riper Park, near Champion in the U.P., is Michigan's coldest place at 38.8°. Grosse Pointe and Monroe are the warmest at 49.9°. For warm summers, try Dearborn, Kalamazoo, Paw Paw, and St. Charles, where July afternoons average 85°. Adrian averages 23 days per summer with temperatures reaching 90°, which most people consider uncomfortably hot. If you can't stand the heat, visit Isle Royale, where the average July daily high temperature is 69°, or live in a houseboat on Lake Superior, where July afternoons average in the 50s and rarely get warmer than 70°. Fayette reaches 90° only every other year, on average, while Isle Royale has seen 90° only once in 50 years! The coldest winters are found at Bergland, in the U.P.'s Porcupine Mountains, where January nighttime lows average -1°. Watersmeet, however, experiences 75 nights below 0° in an average winter, 24 more than Bergland. The mildest January nights are at Detroit and Grand Haven, at 19°, while Detroit, Ludington, Grand Haven, and South Haven average only two nights below 0° per winter. Winter days are

MICHIGAN'S GREATEST HEAT WAVE
Mio, July 1936

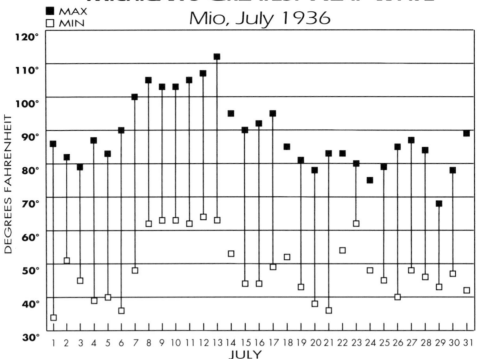

MICHIGAN'S GREATEST COLD WAVE
Vanderbilt, Jan.-Mar. 1954

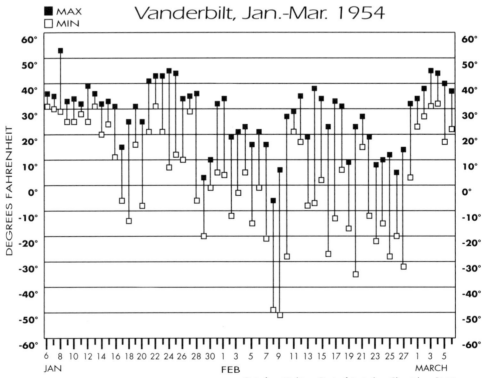

Data from Michigan Dept. of Agriculture-Climatology Division
Michigan State University © A&WGP

warmest at Grosse Pointe, where the average January daily high temperature is an even freezing, 32°. Most of these averages are for the same 30-year period, 1951 through 1980. Comparisons like these should be for the same time period; otherwise, subtle changes in the climate may load the dice in favor of one place over another.

ALL-TIME LOWS AND HIGHS

So much for the averages. Personally, I find the extremes much more interesting, so here goes...

The most extreme low ever seen in Michigan was recorded—where else?—near Vanderbilt on February 9, 1934. (To be precise, back then the readings were made at the Pigeon River Forest ranger station, not far from the trout farm.) A combination of factors turned the 1934 cold wave into a record-setter. First, and most obvious, the air mass was exceptionally cold. For most of January the arctic high kept Alaska in the deep freeze, and Fairbanks recorded its all-time low of -66°. In early February the arctic air poured south, reaching Michigan on February 6. By the morning of February 8, Vanderbilt's temperature stood at -49°, tying the state record set in 1899 at Humboldt. It warmed to -6° during the afternoon, but the winds died down as the sun set, allowing the temperature to plummet. On a clear night, air cools from the ground up, because the ground radiates its heat into space, and the air cools by contact with the ground. Deep snow is an excellent heat radiator, and, like fiberglass batting, insulates the air from the relative warmth of the earth; it even insulates better than organic soils. On this day, Vanderbilt had a foot of snow on the ground. The temperature fell steadily as the clear, still night wore on, reaching -24° shortly after sunset and -51° by dawn. The forest ranger who took the temperature that morning remarked that "the old-timers around here say this is the coldest winter they can remember," and the numbers backed them up. It was Michigan's coldest morning ever. Under a bright sun, Vanderbilt warmed rapidly, and the 27° reading the following afternoon marked a recovery of 78 degrees! The cold wave then slid east, setting all-time records at Buffalo, Boston, Providence, New York City, Philadelphia, along with another state record in New York.

Vanderbilt isn't always the coldest place in Michigan. Fred Nurnberger, Michigan's State Climatologist, has compiled a list of Michigan's coldest places over the past century. Vanderbilt recorded the state's lowest temperature in eight of those hundred years. Other cold spots are Ironwood (seven times) and Watersmeet (ten times). And odd as it may seem, in the year 1892 the honors went to Adrian, a normally mild place in extreme southeastern Michigan. But the true champion is Champion (along with an earlier weather station a few miles away at Humboldt), where Michigan's low was recorded in 26 of the past 100 years.

It also gets hot in Michigan. How hot? Bay City soared to 110° on July 2, 1911, setting a state record that stood for a quarter of a century. That record fell during Michigan's (and the nation's) greatest heat wave of all time, that of July 1936. The month opened on a chilly note, with readings on July 1 as low as 34° at Mio, 45 miles southeast of the Vanderbilt Trout Farm. The heat arrived on July 6, when the mercury touched 90° at several locations (including Mio). The next day temperatures rose to 100° across the state, marking the start of a week of intense heat. Records dropped like flies all week: 105° at Traverse City on July 7, 108° at Flint on July 8, 106° at East Tawas on July 9, 105° at Harbor Beach on July 10, 108° at Vanderbilt on July 11, 106° at Lake City and Onaway on July 12—all record highs that still stand! Saving the best for last, 30 locations saw their hottest day ever on July 13, and seven more on July 14. The thirteenth was the hottest of the lot, with 111° at Saginaw, Newaygo, and Luther exceeding the previous state record. But Mio edged them all out with a top temperature of 112°. That was over half a century ago, but since then no heat wave has come even close to these extremes.

Located in the northern parts of the lower peninsula, Mio may seem an odd place for the

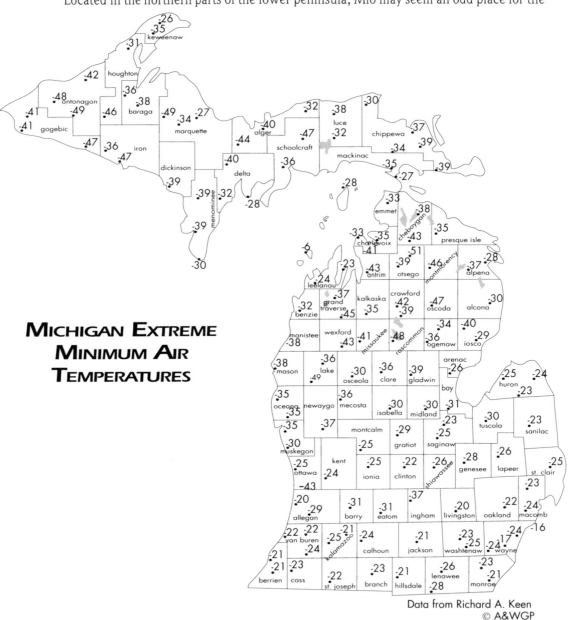

MICHIGAN EXTREME MINIMUM AIR TEMPERATURES

Data from Richard A. Keen
© A&WGP

MICHIGAN EXTREME MAXIMUM AIR TEMPERATURES

Data from Richard A. Keen
© A&WGP

state's hot spot. In the past 100 years, Mio took top honors only three times. In July 1936, Mio's temperatures got a boost from two weeks of clear and rainless weather that made the sandy soil dry as a bone. So, on the afternoon of July 13, rather than evaporating moisture from the ground, the sunshine all went to heating the air.

Most years, Michigan's hottest readings come from the southern counties. Monroe leads the pack, recording the state's high 14 times in 100 years, followed by Adrian with ten. Paw Paw is in fourth place with five, and Owosso and Morenci are tied for fifth with five each. You

January Average Daily Minimum Air Temperature (F°), 1940–1969

Data from Michigan Dept. of Agriculture-Climatology Division, Michigan State University
© A&WGP

may have noticed that I skipped third place; that goes to Marquette, on the shores of chilly Lake Superior, which was the hottest spot in Michigan seven times. Amazingly, a 108° reading at Marquette in 1901 was a state record that stood for ten years! Most of the time Marquette is air-conditioned by Lake Superior, but once in a while, stiff southwest winds replace the cool lake breezes with hot blasts from the plains states. Compressional heating of the air as it descends 900 feet from the plateau just southwest of town adds 5 degrees. In the mountains of the western states, this kind of warm downslope wind is called a "chinook." Some places enjoy the honor of having been both the state's hottest and coldest spots (in different years). Among these are Adrian, Alberta, Atlanta, Cheboygan, Houghton Lake, Mio, and Vanderbilt.

JANUARY AVERAGE DAILY MAXIMUM
AIR TEMPERATURE (F°), 1940–1969

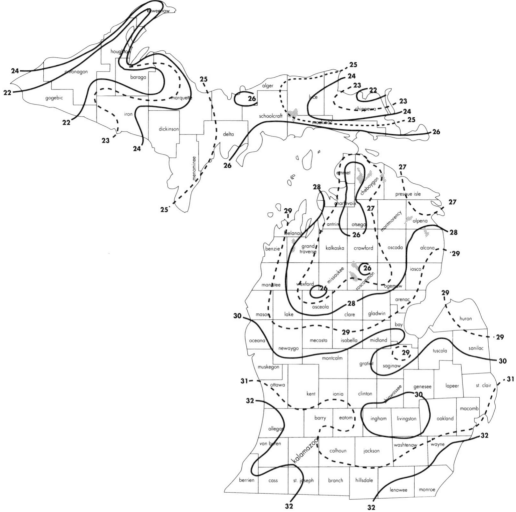

Data from Michigan Dept. of Agriculture-Climatology Division, Michigan State University
© A&WGP

Yep—Michigan's all-time hot spot, Mio, once came in with the year's coldest temperature (in 1941), and four years later Michigan's all-time cold spot, Vanderbilt, was in a six-way tie for the highest reading of the year. So, if you like extremes, Mio and Vanderbilt are your kind of towns. Since record keeping began, each place has experienced temperatures ranging over a span of 159 degrees!

OF TROUT AND TOMATOES

Yet another measure of coldness, and one that means a lot to anyone who grows trees and other perennial plants, is the long-term average of the lowest temperature recorded each winter. The U.S. Department of Agriculture (USDA) has translated these average annual

21

minimum temperatures into "plant hardiness zones" since plants that can handle -10° once or twice a winter may not survive where -20° is recorded. The 1990 USDA. Plant Hardiness Zone Map indicated that Michigan's coldest zone is a small area in the lake-dotted plateau of southern Iron County, along the Wisconsin border near Iron River. In this small area, labeled "Zone 3a," temperatures drop to -35° or -40° in an average winter. That's much too cold for peaches, but intrepid gardeners could try their luck with some hardy stocks of apples, plums, cherries, cranberries, and blueberries. If you want to grow peaches, the only parts of Michigan where you'd have much of a chance are in a narrow band of "Zone 6b" along the shores of Lake Michigan south of Grand Traverse Bay and a patch of southern Macomb County near Lake St. Clair. Within Michigan's "fruit belts," which extend only five or ten miles inland, the winter's low averages between 0° and -5°—the same as parts of Arkansas, Tennessee, and Virginia! When Lake Michigan nearly freezes over, its moderating influences disappear, as happened in 1899 when the mercury dipped to -38° at Ludington and to -43° near Holland. But that kind of cold is extremely rare.

Peaches do just fine along Lake Michigan's shore south of Muskegon, and apple and cherry orchards dot the coast up to Grand Traverse Bay. Not only does the lake moderate the severity of cold waves blowing out of the northwest, it also slows down the onset of spring. That may seem a dubious benefit, but by delaying the blossoming of fruit trees by several weeks the lake gives peach and apple trees a much better chance of surviving a late season freeze. In addition, at the end of summer the now-warm waters of Lake Michigan delay autumn's first freeze, giving fruits several extra weeks to ripen. Most of lower Michigan south of Saginaw Bay lies in "Zone 5b" (winter lows -10° to -15°), while the "fingers of the mitten" and most of the Upper Peninsula have winter lows in the -15° to -30° range. It's the length of summer, not the chill of winter, that matters to growers of annual plants like tomatoes and petunias. The statistic of interest here is the "growing season," the number of days between the average date of the last 32° freeze in spring and the first freeze of fall. Vanderbilt (actually, the trout farm 11 miles east of town; the area is much better for growing trout than tomatoes) doesn't have much of a growing season—it averages only 59 days, from June 21 to August 20. In the U.P., Champion's growing season is 73 days.

Freezing temperatures can happen any time of year at both places, and some years there is no growing season at all. But don't get the impression that all of northern Michigan is an agricultural wasteland. The short growing seasons at Champion and Vanderbilt are rather localized climate freaks, and only 15 miles from both places you'll find growing seasons that are 40 to 50 days longer (110 days at Ishpeming and 112 days at Gaylord). The differences illustrate the agricultural importance of localized variations in soil type and topography. Ishpeming, a mining town, lies on rocky ground, while Champion sits on sandy loam, a mixture of sand and organic soils. The light and relatively fluffy organic soil effectively insulates the air above from heat stored in the ground beneath, allowing the air above to cool faster at night. Both Gaylord and Vanderbilt are on sandy loam soil, but the Vanderbilt Trout Farm is located in a shallow valley along the Pigeon River. This valley is no Grand Canyon, but it is deep enough that pooling cold air lowers Vanderbilt's nighttime temperature by five or ten degrees. At locations where summer temperatures can already dip perilously close to freezing, the effects of soil and topography are enough to push the thermometer below 32°, shortening the growing season by six or seven weeks!

Tomatoes do much better in southern Michigan, especially near the lakes. Michigan's longest growing seasons are found along the shore of southern Lake Michigan and in the extreme southeastern corner of the state. Grand Haven averages 173 consecutive growing days, as do Ypsilanti and Ann Arbor on the other side of the state. Monroe, near Lake Erie, has a 180-day growing season. The average is 140 to 150 growing days per year in places away from the lakes: Lansing, 139 days; Jackson, 151 days; and Battle Creek, 154 days. Michigan's longest growing season, 184 days, is found in Detroit—at City Airport, to be exact (not that anybody grows anything there). Metropolitan gardeners can thank the "urban heat island" for their bigger zucchinis. Heat given off by industries and residences, combined with the previous afternoon's warmth stored in concrete and asphalt, can keep the city five to ten degrees warmer on the clear, calm nights typical of late spring and early fall freezes.

BUT IT FEELS LIKE...

It almost goes without saying that all those numbers you just read about are straight temperatures, read right off a thermometer. Lately there's been a variety of heat and cold indices reported on weather broadcasts and in newspapers, which, while reported in degrees and sounding like temperatures, they are definitely not temperatures. Indeed, these numbers purportedly give a better measure of how much cold or heat we *feel* when we're outside than do ordinary temperatures. The most familiar of these indices is the "wind chill."

The original formula for wind chill factors was developed by Paul Siple. He spent the winter of 1941 at Little America, Antarctica, setting pints of warm water outside and watching them freeze. From the time taken for the pints to freeze in various weather conditions, Siple derived "heat-loss" rates for different combinations of wind speed and temperature. Originally, the heat-loss rates were expressed in kilogram-calories per square meter per hour, but this proved difficult for television weathercasters to say in their five-minute time slots. So the expression "equivalent temperature" was coined. For example, a pint set out on a 5° day with a 45 mile-per-hour wind froze as quickly as one set out at -45° with a 4 m.p.h. wind. Siple chose the 4 m.p.h. wind speed for comparison because he recognized that people are rarely stationary when they're outside in cold weather. Most folks walk briskly, or at least mill smartly, when it's below freezing, giving an effective wind speed of about 4 m.p.h. (the speed of a brisk walk) even when the wind is calm.

Wind chill factors can get quite impressive. On two Sundays in a row, January 10 and January 17, 1982, temperatures around -20° and winds over 40 m.p.h. produced wind chills in excess of -80° in parts of the Upper Peninsula! In general, wind chills below -35° present a real danger of frostbite, prompting the National Weather Service to issue "Wind Chill Advisories." In Russia, where it *really* gets cold, researchers have examined the effect of wind chills in some detail. They taped tiny thermometers on the ears, noses, and cheeks of volunteers, who strolled about in the Siberian cold. At various time intervals, skin temperature

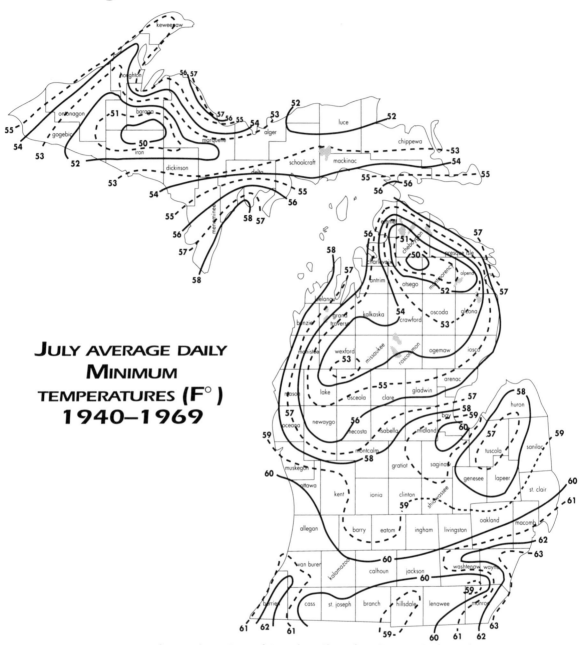

JULY AVERAGE DAILY MINIMUM TEMPERATURES (F°) 1940–1969

Data from Michigan Dept. of Agriculture-Climatology Division, Michigan State University
© A&WGP

was measured. The result was an equation that gives the "face temperature" after 30 minutes outside, and, like the wind chill factor, depends on air temperature and wind speed. Under calm conditions, a -40° air temperature will chill an average face to 32° in 30 minutes, raising the threat of frostbite. Since ears chill faster than the rest of the face, they would be down to 25° by this point). With -80° wind chills like those recorded in the U.P. in January 1982, however, face temperatures will drop to 14° (ears to 7°) in half an hour—obviously, a serious situation. Presumably, the Russian researchers brought their volunteers inside long before their face temperatures reached 9°!

Warm temperatures, of course, tell a different story. When it's 80°, and the wind is still blowing at 40 m.p.h., the wind chill factor computes to be 75°. When it's that warm, however, nobody really cares about wind chills anymore, and the whole idea becomes meaningless

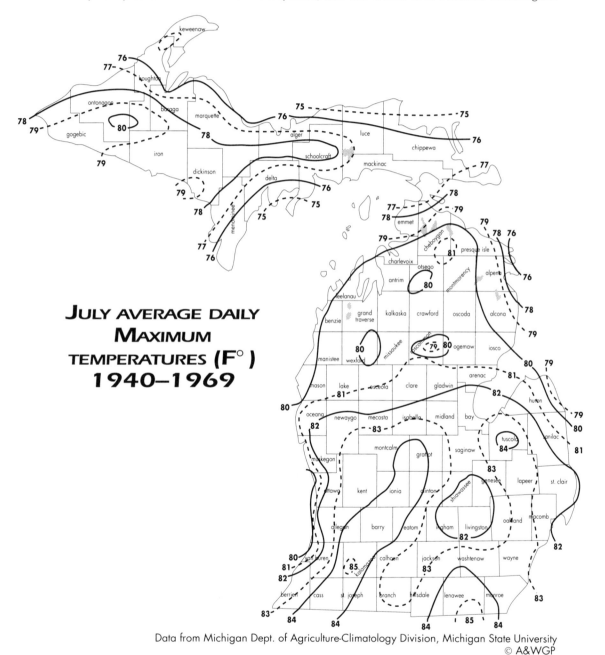

JULY AVERAGE DAILY
MAXIMUM
TEMPERATURES (F°)
1940–1969

Data from Michigan Dept. of Agriculture-Climatology Division, Michigan State University
© A&WGP

25

when the air becomes as warm as your skin (about 91°). During the summer, as they say, "it's not the heat, it's the humidity" that determines outdoor comfort (or discomfort). Actually, it's both heat *and* humidity that come into play. On hot days, skin moisture—sweat—evaporates into the air to cool the body to a comfortable temperature. The lower the humidity, the more rapid the evaporation, and the cooler we feel. On the other hand, with a humidity of 100

MICHIGAN AVERAGE ANNUAL MINIMUM TEMPERATURES
(USDA Plant Hardiness Zones)

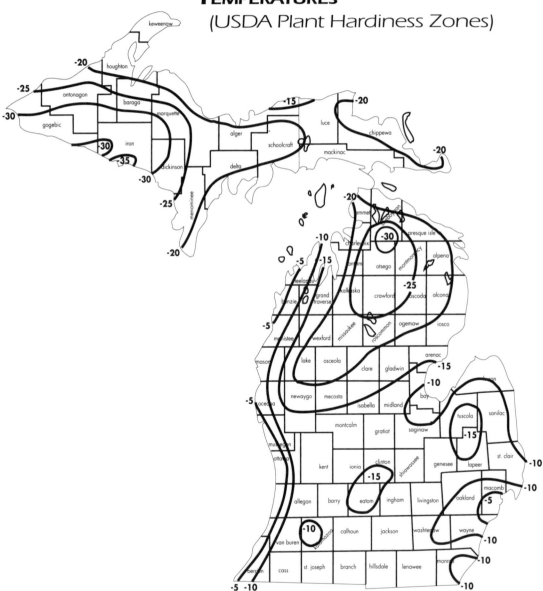

Data from Michigan Dept. of Agriculture-Climatology Division, Michigan State University
© A&WGP

WIND CHILL AND HEAT INDEX TABLES

These tables list wind chills and heat indices for various combinations of actual temperature and wind speed (or relative humidity). They're fairly self-explanatory, but here's a couple of examples: When it's 0° with a 10 m.p.h. wind, 20° with a 45 m.p.h. wind, or -22° with no wind, the wind chill is -22°. Six months later, if it's 85° and the humidity reads 60 percent, the apparent temperature is 90°, but if the humidity is only 20 percent, the apparent temperature is 82°. Asterisks (*) indicate combinations of temperature and humidity that are extremely unlikely (nothing's impossible, though) in Michigan.

WIND CHILL INDEX

ACTUAL TEMPERATURE

WIND SPEED (M.P.H.)	40	30	20	10	0	-10	-20	-30	-40	-50
0-4	40	30	20	10	0	-10	-20	-30	-40	-50
5	37	27	16	6	-5	-15	-26	-36	-47	-57
10	28	16	3	-9	-22	-34	-46	-58	-71	-83
15	23	9	-5	-18	-31	-45	-58	-72	-85	-99
20	19	4	-10	-24	-39	-53	-67	-81	-95	-110
25	16	1	-15	-29	-44	-59	-74	-88	-103	-117
30	13	-2	-18	-33	-49	-64	-79	-93	-109	-123
35	12	-4	-20	-35	-52	-67	-82	-97	-113	-128
40	11	-5	-21	-37	-53	-69	-84	-100	-115	-131
45	10	-6	-22	-38	-54	-70	-85	-102	-117	-133

HEAT INDEX (APPARENT TEMPERATURE)

RELATIVE HUMIDITY	ACTUAL TEMPERATURE									
	70	75	80	85	90	95	100	105	110	115
0	64*	69*	73*	78*	83*	87*	91*	95*	99*	103*
10	65	70	75	80	85	90	95	100	105	111*
20	66	72	77	82	87	93	99	105	112	120*
30	67	73	78	84	90	96	104	113	123	135*
40	68	74	79	86	93	101	110	123	137*	151*
50	69	75	81	88	96	107	120	135*	150*	
60	70	76	83	90	100	114	132*	149*		
70	70	77	85	93	106	124*	144*			
80	71	78	87	97	113*	136*				
90	71	79	89	102*	122*					
100	72	80	91	108*						

percent there is little or no evaporation, and we feel quite muggy. Early heat indices, like the Temperature-Humidity Index (THI) used in the 1960s, reflected the evaporative cooling effect of low humidity by always reading lower than the actual air temperature. So, on a dry 100° day the THI might read 80°. Most folks, however, think of being warmed by humidity, not cooled by dryness, so the THI never really caught on. Now the National Weather Service routinely issues "Apparent Temperatures," or simply the "Heat Index," temperature and humidity combinations to equivalent temperatures at low humidity. The index is based on years of physiological studies, and includes such factors as the person's size, weight, metabolism, clothing, amount of sweating, and body temperature, along with wind, sunshine, and, of course, air temperature and humidity. To simplify matters, the Heat Index is computed for a 5-foot 7-inch, 147-pound person wearing long trousers and a short-sleeved shirt covering 84 percent of the body, with no sunshine and a 5 m.p.h. wind, et cetera, leaving only temperature and humidity to determine the index. With a 35 percent humidity at 105° (rather extreme for Michigan), the Apparent Temperature works out to be 118°, the same index as 130° at 1 percent humidity, or 118° and 14 percent humidity. A more likely heat wave with 95° and 50 percent humidity "feels like" 107° at 17 percent humidity. Note that, unlike the wind chill's 4 m.p.h. wind speed, the reference low humidity is not constant.

What use is the Apparent Temperature? For one, it helps the National Weather Service decide when conditions warrant issuing "heat stress" warnings for people and livestock. At an apparent temperature of 105°, for example, some people may suffer sunstroke or heat exhaustion if they don't take it easy, and a few may undergo heat stroke (a potentially fatal condition). Predicted indices give power companies an idea of how much current will go into air conditioners that day. But apparent temperatures are also a "gee whiz" thing, just like wind chill, that gives folks an opportunity to say, "It felt like 118 degrees," which sounds more impressive than saying, "It was 105 degrees." Neither the wind chill nor the heat index is a temperature. They may *look* like temperatures, since they're given in degrees, but temperatures are what you read from a thermometer—no more and no less. Unfortunately, while these indices provide realistic measures of what the outdoors may feel like, they have been used so much that they are often confused with temperature. Actually, one of these indices is more likely to make its way into a newspaper than the actual temperature. The result is that I've heard people say, "We had 80 below last winter!" They actually believed that the temperature, not the wind chill, was 80 below! The whole idea behind wind chills and heat indices is to improve on simple temperature as an indicator of what it's like outside. Once the indices become confused with temperature, their purpose has been totally defeated. Perhaps they should be used a bit more sparingly.

MICHIGAN WEATHER EXTREMES AND RECORDS

■■■■■■■■■■■■■■■■■■■■■■■■■■■

Michigan has plenty of extremes. Here are some of them:

Geography

Highest place: Mount Curwood, 1,980 feet, or Arvon Mountain, 1,979 feet, depending on whose map you believe. Both are in Baraga County.

Lowest place: Lake Erie, 571 feet.

Temperature (averages based on 1951-80)

Warmest place: Grosse Pointe and Monroe, annual average 49.9°.

Coldest place: Van Riper Park, near Champion, annual average 38.8°.

Hottest summer days: Dearborn, Kalamazoo, Paw Paw, and St. Charles, average July daily maximum 85°.

Coldest winter nights: Bergland, average January daily minimum -1°.

Hottest ever: 112° at Mio, July 13, 1936.

Coldest ever: -51° at Pigeon River Forest (near Vanderbilt), February 8, 1934. (An unofficial and unverified -55° was reported at Fort Brady, near Sault Ste. Marie, February 13 and February 14, 1875)

Warmest month: August 1947, average 81.9° at Dowagiac.

Coldest month: January 1912, average -7.2° at Watersmeet.

Warmest year, statewide average (since 1888): 1921, averaged 48.3°.

Coldest year, statewide average (since 1888): 1917, averaged 40.9°. (1875 had an approximate statewide average of 40.1°, based on fewer stations.)

Longest heat wave (daily maximum over 100°): 9 days, Kalamazoo, July 7-15, 1936.

Longest cold wave (daily maximum below 0°): 8 days, Ewen, February 4-11, 1899.

Longest cold wave (nights 0° or below): 35 days, Bessemer, January 19 to February 22, 1936.

Warmest night: 82° overnight minimum at Holland and South Haven, August 17, 1988.

Coldest day: -21° daytime maximum at Ironwood, January 17, 1982.

Shortest average growing season: 59 days, June 21 to August 20, Vanderbilt.

Longest average growing season: 184 days, April 22 to October 24, Detroit. (Growing seasons are measured from the average date of the last 32° temperature in spring to the first freeze in fall.)

Warmest lake water: 86°, western Lake Erie, August 2, 1988.

MICHIGAN WEATHER EXTREMES

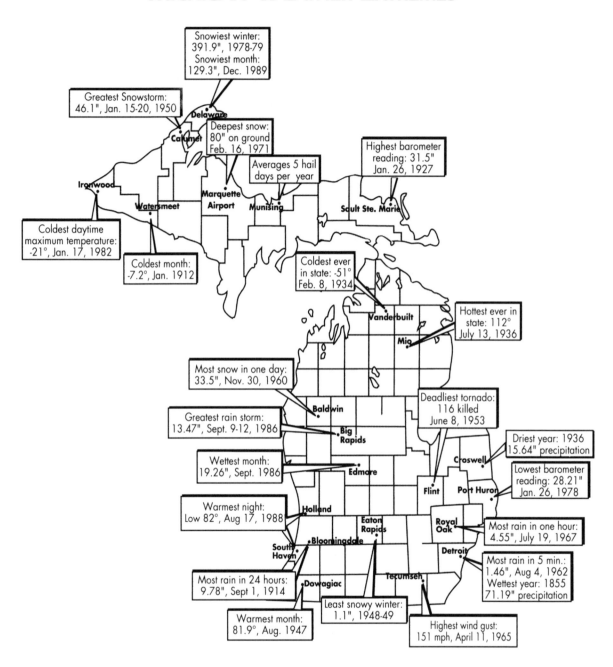

Snowiest winter:
391.9", 1978-79
Snowiest month:
129.3", Dec. 1989

Greatest Snowstorm:
46.1", Jan. 15-20, 1950

Deepest snow:
80" on ground
Feb. 16, 1971

Averages 5 hail
days per year

Highest barometer
reading: 31.5"
Jan. 26, 1927

Coldest daytime
maximum temperature:
-21°, Jan. 17, 1982

Coldest month:
-7.2°, Jan. 1912

Coldest ever
in state: -51°
Feb. 8, 1934

Hottest ever in
state: 112°
July 13, 1936

Most snow in one day:
33.5", Nov. 30, 1960

Deadliest tornado:
116 killed
June 8, 1953

Greatest rain storm:
13.47", Sept. 9-12, 1986

Driest year: 1936
15.64" precipitation

Wettest month:
19.26", Sept. 1986

Lowest barometer
reading: 28.21"
Jan. 26, 1978

Warmest night:
Low 82°, Aug 17, 1988

Most rain in one hour:
4.55", July 19, 1967

Most rain in 24 hours:
9.78", Sept 1, 1914

Most rain in 5 min.:
1.46", Aug 4, 1962
Wettest year: 1855
71.19" precipitation

Warmest month:
81.9°, Aug. 1947

Least snowy winter:
1.1", 1948-49

Highest wind gust:
151 mph, April 11, 1965

Delaware · Calumet · Ironwood · Watersmeet · Marquette Airport · Munising · Sault Ste. Marie · Vanderbuilt · Mio · Baldwin · Big Rapids · Croswell · Edmore · Flint · Port Huron · Holland · Eaton Rapids · Royal Oak · Detroit · South Haven · Bloomingdale · Dowagiac · Tecumseh

Data from Richard A. Keen
© A&WGP

30

Precipitation (averages based on 1951-80)

Wettest place: 39.16", Niles.
Driest place: 26.00", Sebewaing.
Most precipitation in one year: 71.19" at Detroit, 1855.
Least precipitation in one year: 15.64" at Croswell, 1936.
Most rain in 5 minutes: 1.46" at Detroit, August 4, 1962.
Most rain in one hour: 4.55" at Royal Oak, July 19, 1967.
Most rain in 24 hours: 9.78" at Bloomingdale, September 1, 1914.
Greatest storm: 13.47" at Big Rapids, September 9-12, 1986.
Wettest month: 19.26", Edmore, September 1986.
Wettest year, statewide (since 1888): 1930, averaged 39.56".
Driest year, statewide (since 1888): 1985, averaged 22.31".
Wettest month, statewide (since 1888): September, 1986, averaged 8.62".
Driest month, statewide (since 1888): March, 1910, averaged 0.25".

Snow

Snowiest place: Delaware, averages 241.5" per winter.
Least snowiest place: Grosse Pointe, averages 28.7" per winter.
Most snow in one day: 33.5" at Baldwin, November 30, 1960.
Most snow in a single storm: 46.1", Calumet, January 15-20, 1950 (6 days).
Most snow in one month: 129.3" at Delaware, December 1989.
Most snow in one winter: 391.9" at Delaware, 1978-79.
Least snow in one winter: 1.1" at Eaton Rapids, 1948-49.
Greatest depth of snow on ground: 80" at Marquette Airport, February 16, 1971.

Hail

Largest stone: 4-inch diameter stones fell at Stony Point, near Monroe, on March 27, 1991.
Greatest accumulation: 24" (in drifts) near Yale, St. Clair County, July 5, 1968.
Most: Munising averaged 5.1 hailstorms per year (mostly small stones), 1901-1960.
Least: Sault Ste. Marie and Monroe average fewer than 1.5 hailstorms per year.

Sunshine

Sunniest place: Detroit averages 2,365 hours of sunshine per year, or 54 percent of total possible.
Cloudiest place: Houghton averages 1,840 hours of sunshine per year, or 42 percent of total possible.

Barometric Pressure (reduced to sea level)

Highest: 31.15" at Sault Ste. Marie, January 26, 1927.
Lowest: 28.21" at Port Huron, January 26, 1978 (lower pressures have undoubtedly occurred in tornadoes).

Wind (fastest measured speeds)

95 m.p.h. at Detroit, June 1890 (highest wind at a major weather station).
109 m.p.h. on Lake Huron, August 6, 1965 (highest wind reported by a ship on the Lakes).
151 m.p.h. at Tecumseh Airport, April 11, 1965, on the southern edge of a large tornado. Winds near the center of the tornado reached an estimated 240 m.p.h.

260+ m.p.h. (estimated) in tornadoes near Flint on June 8, 1953; Grand Rapids on April 3, 1956; and at Ortonville and Oakwood on May 25, 1896.

Lightning

Most damaging: Lightning set a $5 million blaze at the Swedish Crucible Steel Co. in Hamtramck on May 22, 1970.

Most injuries by a single event: 90 at a campground near Lansing, August 23, 1975, by a sudden outburst of at least 6 lightning strikes.

Most catastrophic: Two people killed, four injured, and $50,000 damage by a single lightning strike at Detroit in August 1964.

Tornadoes

First recorded: Detroit (February 1834) and Kalamazoo (October 18, 1834).

Deadliest: June 8, 1953, Genesee and Lapeer counties (near Flint), 116 killed.

Most in one year: 39 in 1974.

Most in one day: 16 on April 11, 1965 (Palm Sunday).

Longest path: 90 miles (81 in Michigan), from Lake Pleasant, Indiana, to near Waltz, Wayne County, on April 11, 1965.

Widest path: 6,000 feet, in the same tornado noted above. This tornado may have been three miles wide when it passed between Clinton and Tecumseh.

Strongest: Tornadoes near Flint on June 8, 1953, Grand Rapids on April 3, 1956, and Ortonville to Oakwood on May 25, 1896, had winds exceeding 260 m.p.h. (estimated from damage reports).

Smallest: Several brief touchdowns with paths no wider than 10 feet have been reported.

Most damaging outbreak: $51 million, April 11, 1965.

Average path length: 5 miles.

Average width: 322 feet.

Average wind speed: 83 m.p.h.

Most average: A perfectly "average" tornado is a statistical impossibility. Probably the closest thing was a tornado near Rankin on July 25, 1986. Its path was 5.7 miles long and 225 feet wide, and peak winds were in the 73-112 m.p.h. range. It destroyed a barn.

Natural Disasters

Most lives lost: Estimated 200 killed in extensive forest fires, October 8-10, 1871.

Forest fires in The Thumb took 169 lives, August 30-September 7, 1881.

Greatest damage: $400 million in flash floods across central Lower Michigan, September 9 to September 11, 1986.

NOTE: These record highs, lows, mosts, and leasts for Michigan come from a wide variety of sources. No doubt there are a few even more extreme records out there—including some "unofficial" and unpublished extremes—that I missed. Let me know if you hear of any!

SUMMER STORMS

■ ■

Winter is a fun time of year, with all sorts of enjoyable activities—skating, sledding, skiing, ice fishing, shoveling, driving—to keep our minds off the fact that we're cold. Most folks seem to enjoy winter, but by March nearly all (even if they won't admit it) have grown a little tired (or plenty sick) of it, and start looking forward to spring. Spring approaches with melting snow and ice breaking up in lakes, and arrives with robins and tiny green leaves bursting from tree buds. But to those who look to the skies to follow the seasons, one of the sweetest sounds in all of nature is that first distant rumble of thunder on a balmy April afternoon. The first thunderstorm of the year doesn't have to come in April, mind you. It's just as likely to show up in March, and some years there's the odd wintertime thunderstorm (or thunder-snow storm). Sometimes you have to wait until May for that first boom of spring, although by then the thunderstorm season is usually in high gear.

Once or twice a week, on the average, from April through September, Michiganders are treated to the wonder and spectacle of thunder, lightning, and general commotion of these storms. It's less of a treat, of course, if your house is struck by lightning or damaging winds, but for the most part thunderstorms bring welcome rains when they're needed the most— during the crop-growing season. The annual number of thunderstorms in Michigan usually ranges from about 50 at Grand Rapids to 36 at Houghton. A more commonly recorded statistic is the number of *days* with thunderstorms, or "thunderstorm days." This total runs around 35 to 40 across the western half of lower Michigan and around 25 or 30 in the U.P. (some days have two or more storms). For comparison, there are 100 thunderstorm days in central Florida and up to 80 in parts of the Rocky Mountains in Colorado and New Mexico. On the other extreme, Sacramento, California, averages but one thunderstorm day per year, and along the Arctic coast of Alaska, Point Barrow gets about one thunderstorm per decade. Now while, anything that happens 35 to 55 times per year may seem commonplace., consider this: the average thunderstorm goes on for about an hour, so the 44 storms that rattle Detroit each year last a total of 44 hours (approximately). So, out of the 8,760 hours in a year, only 44—or one-half of one percent—are occupied by thunderstorms. That means that 99.5 percent of the time there *are no* thunderstorms!

Meteorologically speaking, thunderstorms are actually quite rare, and require a very special set of circumstances to take place, a state called "instability." Instability means the atmosphere is unstable. Examples of unstable situations abound in the world around us—a rock perched on a ledge, a cocked gun, an egg balanced on its end, a loaded mouse trap—all ready to go off at the slightest provocation. In each case, the effect exceeds the immediate cause, and once the reaction is triggered and the energy is spent, the situation (usually) becomes stable (at least for a while). Since the world abounds with little provocations, most unstable situations don't last very long, and most of the time, most things are stable. (So much for the analogies—let's get back to thunderstorms.)

Normally, the atmosphere is stable. Cold air in a valley—an inversion—is stable, since the cold air is on the bottom. Cold air is "heavier," or more accurately, denser (meaning more air molecules per cubic foot), than warm air. In essence, the "lighter" warm air floats on top of the cold air—it's the same thing that keeps hot air balloons up. If you try to lift some cold air off the ground, say, 100 feet, you'll find that it will be surrounded by warmer, lighter air. Let it go, and the cold air sinks back to the valley floor. Rising currents don't go very far in stable air. With unstable air, however, the temperature drops off fairly rapidly with height—about 25° Fahrenheit per mile. If a blob of air is lifted off the ground, it expands and cools as the pressure around it decreases. Despite the cooling, the lifted blob remains warmer than the air around it, and keeps going up. Instability is even stronger if there's water vapor in the air to release its latent heat. If you give an upward kick to air in an unstable air layer, it continues to soar upwards in a relatively warm stream. If the air is moist enough, the rising air stream may become a thunderstorm. As it rises, expands, and cools, water vapor in the air condenses into tiny droplets of liquid water, and a cloud is born. The condensation of gaseous water vapor into liquid water actually heats up the air in our blob. This is the opposite of evaporation, when liquid water cools its surroundings as it evaporates into vapor (if you've ever stepped out of a swimming pool on a breezy day, you know what I mean). Warming the blob makes it rise a little bit faster.

By now, I'll bet you can see where this is headed—as the blob rises faster, there's more condensation, causing it to rise faster yet, and so on. We see these rising blobs as growing cauliflower clouds. Back near the ground, more moist air is drawn into the base of the cloud to keep the condensation going. This process of rising, condensation, heating and faster rising currents is called "convection." Like combustion in the cylinders of a car engine, it's what keeps thunderstorms going. There are many ways to provoke an unstable atmosphere into making a thunderstorm, all of which involve some initial upward shove that starts the cycle of condensation, rising currents, and convection. For many thunderstorms, the updrafts begin with air heated by the sunlit ground below (these are your typical scattered afternoon thundershowers). Some storms, though, get their kick from the up-and-down air currents in different sections of cyclones, especially where the cold front wedges under the moist air and shoves it upward or along the warm front, where the humid air rides up and over the cold air. These "frontal" thunderstorms (ones that form along warm or cold fronts) are often the most severe, sometimes bringing hail, high winds, and tornadoes. Virtually all winter thunderstorms are "frontal."

ANNUAL MEAN PRECIPITATION
(Inches) 1940-1969

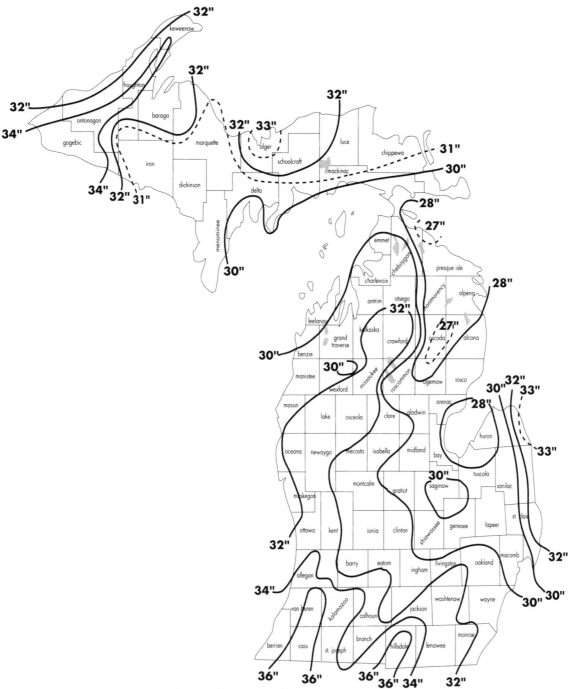

Data from Michigan Dept. of Agriculture-Climatology Division, Michigan State University
© A&WGP

MICHIGAN STATEWIDE AVERAGE PRECIPITATION
Annual and 20-Year Averages, 1888-1992

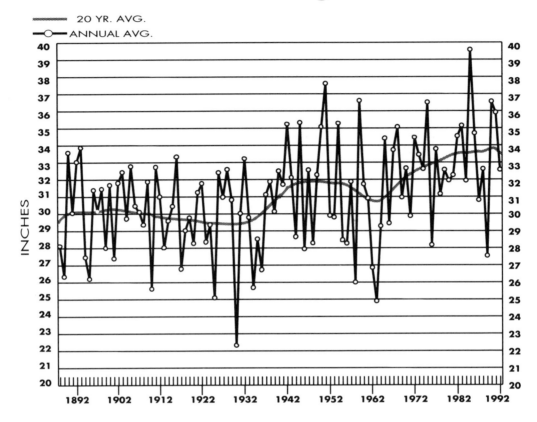

MICHIGAN AVERAGE MONTHLY PRECIPITATION

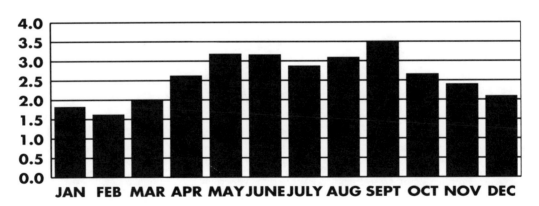

Fronts and sunlight are the intuitively most obvious ways to start a thunderstorm, but many have more esoteric causes. For example, many thunderstorms don't get going until the sun goes down. This is especially true in southern Michigan, where more thunderstorms occur at night than during the day (the hourly peak is around 4 A.M.). The cause here is the exact opposite of the solar-powered daytime thunderstorms: clouds and haze layers several miles up radiate their heat out to space, cooling the atmosphere at cloud-top level. Cooling aloft at night has the same effect as heating the ground by day, namely, the atmosphere becomes unstable and air starts rising. Many times both processes go on, with the sun "priming" the atmosphere during the afternoon and the nighttime cloud-top cooling finally setting the storms off a few hours after sundown. The result can be some real doozies. Those caught beneath one of these storms get lots of rain and little sleep, while neighbors in the next county sit on their porches and watch "heat lightning" light up the sky.

Some late summer and early fall thunderstorms start when cool air crosses one of the still-warm Great Lakes, picking up warmth and moisture in their lower layers and becoming somewhat unstable. Michigan's hail capital, Munising, owes its fame to storms set off by the relative warmth of Lake Superior during the fall months. Three of Munising's annual average of five hailstorms occur during September, October, and November. While that sounds like a lot of hail, the hail is usually quite small and rarely damaging, and some of the November "hail" storms are probably "snow pellets"—soft, BB-size snowballs that couldn't hurt a flea. Sometimes several sources of instability can combine forces to generate some unusual effects. There have been cases of winter lake-effect snow squalls which, in combination with a passing cold front, produced tornadoes! September has produced some of Michigan's heaviest rains and worst floods, probably because of the extra kick given to otherwise mediocre storms by the warm lakes.

Like the rest of us mortals, thunderstorms have life cycles of birth, growth, the prime of their lives, and death. Many of the meanest storms start out as a cotton-like "cumulus" clouds that look like little lambs loitering in the sky. If the air is moist and unstable enough, and the right trigger comes along, one of these puffy cumulus clouds starts growing into a billowing cauliflower, or "towering cumulus." The atmosphere gets colder as you go higher, and three or four miles up (lower in the winter) the temperature drops below freezing. Now ice crystals, rather than liquid water droplets, result from condensation. The top of the cauliflower cloud assumes the fuzzy and fibrous appearance characteristic of ice clouds. High winds aloft may whip ice crystals from the main cloud into a flat, spreading cap often called an "anvil" cloud. With the appearance of ice crystals, the growing cloud becomes an entirely new animal. Ice crystals are much more efficient than water droplets at grabbing moisture from the air, and are even quite capable of stealing moisture from the droplets themselves. The ice crystals grow rapidly, eventually becoming snowflakes that fall and melt into rain. Virtually all of Michigan's rain—even that which turns to steam when it lands on a baking-hot street—starts out as snow! Now that it's raining, we can add the Latin word "nimbus" (meaning rain) to our cumulus cloud, and call the cloud a "cumulonimbus." ZAP! The cumulonimbus cloud is not just a cloud; it's a storm. And not just a storm, but a thunderstorm!

Thunder (and lightning) result from the same ice crystals that make most of the rain. For some poorly understood reason, when liquid water droplets freeze into ice, electrical charges develop. Ice crystals become positively charged, while the remaining liquid droplets take on a negative charge. Soon the whole cloud becomes charged. Positive charges collect in the icy cloud top and negative charges accumulate in the lower, warmer parts of the cloud. Normally the ground is also negatively charged, but the concentration of electrons in the lower cloud repels the negative ground charge (like charges repel; opposites attract), leaving a positively charged ground directly beneath the cloud. The gathering electrical charges build voltages as high as 100 million volts within the cloud and between cloud and ground.

Air is pretty good at holding electrical charges apart. In clouds, air can separate voltages at the rate of 3,000 volts per foot, or 15 million volts per mile. When 100 million volts show up, however, sparks fly. First a relatively weak and invisible "leader stroke" makes its way down from the base of the cloud. One-hundredth of a second later the leader stroke reaches a tree, antenna, the ground, or sometimes several targets, and an electrical pathway—a wire of sorts—connects the cloud and ground. A massive "return stroke" shoots up along the leader path at one-sixth the speed of light. Return strokes may rise from each of several ground targets to join several hundred feet up, forming branched lightning. The concentration of electricity in a path a few inches across heats the air almost instantaneously to tens of thousands of degrees—several times hotter (and brighter) than the surface of the sun! We see the glowing channel as lightning, while the sudden heating and expansion of the air—essentially a mile-long explosion—makes thunder.

The sight and sound of lightning and thunder are produced simultaneously, but light zips along at 186,000 miles per second, much faster than sound's slow 1,000 *feet* per second (or one mile in five seconds). You see lightning a fraction of a blink after it happens, but the rumble of thunder may takes several (or many) seconds to reach your ears. This gap allows you to do some low-tech meteorology. Count the number of seconds between the flash and the boom, divide by five, and you've got your distance from the storm in miles. Do this every few minutes and you can deduce whether the storm is moving towards or away from you, and even predict when it will arrive.

There are different kinds of lightning. We're most familiar with "cloud-to-ground" lightning, which, of course, zaps from the cloud to the ground. Ninety percent of all lightning, however, stays inside the cloud, and is know as (naturally) "inside cloud" lightning. There's also "cloud-to-cloud" lightning that connects oppositely charged parts of two different clouds. Those diffuse flashes in the sky popularly known as "heat" (or "sheet") lightning are simply the reflection by clouds and air of ordinary lightning too distant to be seen directly. Finally, there's the newly-discovered (by lightning detector networks) "positive" lightning that goes from positively-charged icy cloud tops to the negatively-charged ground several miles away from the storm. Positive lightning is particularly deceptive because it can appear to come out of a clear sky, literally a "bolt from the blue." Also, since the bolts come from the cloud top, not the base, they have to travel farther and are proportionally more energetic. This "new" kind of lightning is something to think about when the sun comes out and a rainbow appears, but the storm is still only a few miles away.

All lightning uses a lot of energy and uses it very quickly. For a few millionths of a second the *instantaneous* peak rate of energy usage may exceed a trillion watts, equivalent to the *average* consumption rate of the entire United States. But lightning strokes are incredibly brief, and the *total* electrical energy expended by an average lightning flash is several hundred kilowatt hours. If you were to buy lightning from Consumers Power, it would cost about $50 per flash. Networks of lightning detectors have found that an average square mile of Michigan is struck by lightning about 10 or 15 times a year. That means Michigan's 58,216 square miles are peppered by 700,000 strikes a year, or about $35 million worth of electricity.

A total of 672 Michiganders were struck by lightning between 1959 and 1990, according to the National Climate Data Center. This statistic includes 88 deaths and 584 reported injuries, but there are undoubtedly many unreported minor injuries and quite a few good scares. Factor in the population of Michigan (9 million) and our average life span (75 years or so), and your odds of being struck by lightning sometime in your life are one in 6,000. Now you can put a number behind the proverbial "about as likely as getting hit by lightning." Many of those killed and injured by lightning were engaged in outdoor activities such as boating and swimming (26 reported in 32 years), golfing (31), and working near tractors or road equipment (15). One hundred one Michiganders were struck while standing beneath trees, but the greatest number (219) were hit by lightning in open fields or baseball parks. Ninety people were hurt, one seriously, on August 23, 1975, when lightning repeatedly struck a campground near Lansing, and 45 National Guardsmen were slightly injured by lightning that struck the radio tent at their camp near Grayling on June 20, 1979. However, even some indoor activities can be dangerous during a thunderstorm—17 people talking on the telephone have been hit by lightning coming "over the wires." These statistics give a pretty clear idea of what *not* to do during thunderstorms.

STORMY WEATHER

Continuing with the saga of our storm, the thunderstorm is now crackling with lightning and dropping some rain. It is now also capable of producing some of Michigan's most destructive weather. While the cumulus was growing, its air currents were all heading upward. But as rain begins to fall, so does some of the air. When the rain-laden downdrafts reach the ground, they spread out, and we enjoy the first gusts of cool air that break the heat on an August afternoon. Sometimes, though, these gusts can get out of hand and exceed 100 m.p.h., wrecking roofs and toppling trees. On other occasions the downdrafts may be concentrated in a column less than a mile (sometimes only a few hundred yards) across. The powerful downdraft hits the ground like a garden hose spraying a wall, spreading out in all directions at speeds of 50 to 100 m.p.h. or even higher. People and things on the ground experience sudden, localized, short-lived, and rapidly changing winds—a brief tempest known as a "microburst." On the ground microbursts can cause severe local damage that mimics that of a tornado, but the greatest peril is to aircraft flying through the shifting winds. Several recent airline disasters (none in Michigan) have been attributed to microbursts. Experimental weather detection systems, including wind gauge networks and Doppler radar (which can pick up motions in the atmosphere) are due to be installed at many airports during the 1990s, making the skies a safer place.

Most of the rain the falls from a thunderstorm reaches the ground in short order. Some raindrops, however, stray from the downdraft and get caught in a nearby updraft. These drops blow back up to the cold parts of the cloud, where they freeze into hail. The frozen drop may then fall to the ground, or it may fall a while, picking up moisture along the way, and once again get blown back up to the top of the cloud. This cycle can repeat as long as the updrafts are strong enough to lift the growing hailstone. With updrafts approaching 100 miles an hour in some storms, the hail can grow quite large before dropping out. A baseball-size hailstone riding hurricane-force winds packs the wallop of a major league fastball—something crops and windows are no match for.

Eventually, the supply of moist air that feeds the storm runs out, and the thunderstorm begins to fade. Updrafts within the cloud weaken and finally cease, leaving only sinking currents of rain- and snow-filled air. The cloud's edges turn ragged as they begin to evaporate. Above, the icy anvil cloud may separate and blow off with the high-level winds, while below, light rain falls out of a disappearing cloud.

The typical life cycle of growth, storm, and decay runs one to three hours. Not all storms fade so fast. Thunderstorms pushed along by cold fronts are continually shoved into the moist air mass, while some slow-moving storms may tap a steady flow of moisture blowing in from afar. In either case the action can go on for many hours or the better part of a day. Some of the longest-lived thunderstorms line up like halfbacks and march forward into the moist air, scooping up fresh water vapor as they go. The approach of one of these "squall lines" can be an imposing spectacle, with a wall of dark, thundering clouds stretching from horizon to horizon. Squall lines often develop along cold fronts, but may outrun the front and take off on their own. Other thunderstorms may congregate in enormous "Mesoscale Convective Complexes," or MCCs (maybe someday we'll have a snazzier name). An MCC may grow one or two hundred miles across and live 12 to 24 hours, with new thunderstorms continually popping up to replace old, dying storms. The total rainfall from one of these systems can exceed that of a hurricane, and MCCs have unleashed more than one flash flood on Michigan's waterways.

TORNADO!

■ ■

"Mama, is the sky going to scream at us tonight?"
Mary Ann, a 3-year-old survivor of the 1953 Flint tornado

Around dusk every year on June 8, a small crowd gathers in front of a small memorial at Beecher High School, on Coldwater Road just north of Flint. They pause to remember friends and family lost decades ago—at 8:30 P.M. on Monday, June 8, 1953—when a two-block-wide tornado turned their quiet residential neighborhood into splinters. It struck while many families were relaxing after dinner, and the storm was particularly cruel in its choice of victims—nearly half of the 115 dead were children. Nine hundred people were injured, and hundreds of houses were destroyed. But the statistics can't even hint at the frantic horror of those fleeing a drive-in theater as the tornado bore down on them, or the anguish of night-shift workers who rushed home from Flint's factories to find their homes and families gone.

Michigan's worst tornado started as a 50-foot wide "dancing funnel" with spinning "fingers" that touched down in a pasture near Coldwater and Linden Roads, where it turned over some clumps of grass. The twister grew in size and strength and lost its funnel shape as it headed east, and during its three-minute rampage down Coldwater Road and Kurtz Avenue it was described as a swirling, debris-filled mass of grayish-blue and black smoke. Survivors told of huge elm and maple trees ripped from the ground, of cars flying past their windows, and of houses flung intact across streets and shattering against trees. Many saw "bright balls of fire" inside the funnel—something seen only in the mightiest tornadoes. The incredible roar was likened to that of a furnace, freight trains on a trestle, and even a giant pencil sharpener!

After flattening the Coldwater Road area, the tornado continued east into Lapeer County, where it destroyed several farms. After one hour and 27 miles on the ground, the tornado dissipated, but as it did, its parent thunderstorm immediately spawned another equally large, but fortunately much less devastating, tornado a few miles to the south. The second tornado tracked east to Lakeport and out over Lake Huron, while the massive thunderstorm responsible for it all continued into Canada. Debris fell all along the path of the storm, including a 16-foot aluminum house trailer found eight miles from its original home, textbooks tossed 35

41

NUMBER OF TORNADOES PER CENTURY
Passing within 5 miles

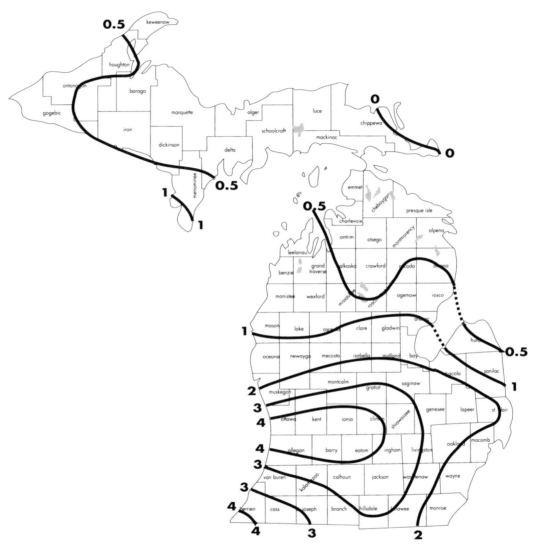

miles from the Beecher School, and canceled checks that sailed 200 miles into Ontario. A dime had a much shorter journey—it was found implanted like a bullet in the stump of a tree.

Tornadoes are not only the most powerful storms on earth; they are frightening, fascinating, deadly, beautiful, and quirky. Fortunately, they are also rare, and require very special meteorological conditions to develop. Among these are moist low-level air overrun by drier air aloft, strong instability, a strong jet stream aloft, a change in wind direction and speed between the lower and upper levels of the troposphere, and some preexisting rotation in the lowest layers of air. All of these conditions may be found in the warm sectors of strong cyclones, while a sufficient number of these conditions to generate tornadoes might be found elsewhere.

Like nowhere else on earth, these special conditions are found in the central part of the United States in an area known as "Tornado Alley." More than half of the world's annual average of 1,000 tornadoes touch down in the central United States, making the tornado more American than baseball and hot dogs! Over the past century tornadoes have killed between 15,000 and 20,000 Americans, but deaths have decreased in recent years, thanks to improved forecasting and warning systems. During the 1980s, tornadoes were responsible for an average of 60 deaths per year. Meanwhile, property damage due to tornadoes has steadily increased to an annual loss of $1 billion or more in most years since 1973.

Michigan lies on the very northeastern fringe of Tornado Alley. With an average of 16 tornadoes per year since 1953, Michigan ranks twentieth in the nation (right behind Minnesota and just ahead of Ohio). Compared to global statistics, those 16 tornadoes are more than Australia's 14 and Japan's 11 tornadoes per year, and not a whole lot less than the 25 or so per year reported from Italy, New Zealand and Great Britain. The southern half of the Lower Peninsula records the most—and the worst—of Michigan's tornadoes. Some counties—like Berrien, Genesee, Lenawee, Monroe, and Wayne—average nearly one tornado per year. When the tornadoes' sizes and path lengths (and area affected) are factored in along with their sheer numbers, the most tornado-prone counties turn out to be Allegan, Barry, Eaton, Ionia, Kent, and Ottawa. That puts the center of Michigan's tornado belt between Grand Rapids and Hastings. Of course, this is based on the past performance of tornadoes that have visited Michigan. There is no guarantee that future tornadoes will favor the same locations.

The frequency of tornadoes drops off rapidly as one heads north across the state. While every county in Michigan has reported at least one tornado, a home north of a Saginaw-Muskegon line is only about one-fifth as likely to be hit by a tornado as is a house south of that line (which, of course, is where most of Michigan's houses are!). The Upper Peninsula is even less prone to tornadic wrath—only 10 percent of Michigan's tornadoes touch down north of the Mackinac Straits. Places like Seattle, not known for such things, have been visited by more tornadoes than most U.P. counties!

To everything there is a season, and for tornadoes the seasons to be wary are spring and summer. This is when the conducive conditions of warmth, humidity, winds aloft, and so on are most likely to occur together. Thirteen of the year's 16 tornadoes (on the average) touch down from April through August, with the peak months—June and July—hosting six of them. Summer tornadoes tend to be smaller and weaker than their springtime cousins, and 64 percent of Michigan's strong tornadoes (the ones you really need to worry about) have occurred in April, May, and June. Tornadoes are late risers, too, and very few are seen before noon. Only 13 percent of all Michigan tornadoes occur between midnight and noon, while the peak hours of 2 P.M. to 9 P.M. (Eastern Standard Time) catch 73 percent of the total. The hour from 4 to 5 P.M. accounts for 13 percent of Michigan's tornadoes. The reason is, of course, that the sun heats the lower atmosphere during the day, making it hotter, lighter, more unstable, and ready to rise.

So now it's 5 P.M. on a June afternoon, and Michigan lies in the warm sector of a late spring cyclone approaching from the west. All the conditions are ripe for tornado development, and

Michigan Tornadoes
Average for each month

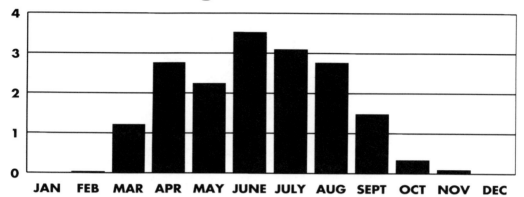

Data from National Oceanographic and Atmospheric Administration © A&WGP

the National Weather Service has issued a Tornado Watch. Somewhere in Michigan, a thunderstorm is born. Its powerful updrafts (due to moisture and instability) draw in the slowly rotating air circulating around the cyclone. This concentrates the spinning motion, like water swirling faster as it approaches a drain. As the updraft strengthens, the spinning speeds up, until the updraft becomes a narrow, rotating column—a tornado. In exceptional cases, the whole thunderstorm may start rotating, becoming a parent cloud capable of spawning tornadoes every few minutes for an hour or more. These awesome "supercell" thunderstorms ravage the Midwest many times every year, and are responsible for the most lethal tornadoes. Once or twice a decade, a springtime cyclone heading east from the Rockies spawns supercells and tornadoes by the dozen on its march to sea. The ensuing atmospheric reign of terror may spread devastation across an area of several states and leave hundreds dead and thousands injured. Most of Michigan's worst tornadoes have been offspring of these enormous atmospheric rampages.

Tornadoes come in many sizes, shapes and strengths. The largest can be a mile or more across with 300-mile-per-hour winds, and may scour the land along a 50- to 250-mile path before dissipating. Fortunately, these mile-wide monsters are rare, but when they strike, it's a mess. During the Palm Sunday tornado outbreak in 1965, a huge tornado cleared out a 1.5-mile path across Grant and Stevens counties. At the other extreme, tiny twisters may touch down for a few seconds, damaging a single tree or part of a roof before disappearing. I saw one leave a neat but narrow 30-foot-wide path in a cornfield, and another with winds barely strong enough to pick up cardboard boxes (although it sent newspapers spiralling thousands of feet up into the base of the thunderstorm!).

The typical Michigan tornado, based on statistics gathered by the National Severe Storms Forecast Center in Kansas City, has winds of 83 m.p.h. swirling around a 300-foot-wide funnel, and moves at 40 m.p.h. over a five-mile-long path during its five- or 10-minute lifetime. Like the 1.9-child family, though, this "typical" tornado is actually the rarest of them all.

The appearance of a tornado can vary as much as its size, ranging from fat cylinders to thin, coiling ropes. The famous funnel cloud results from the condensation of water vapor inside the rotating column, where the pressure and temperature are lower. If the funnel cloud doesn't reach all the way to the ground, the rotating tube of air may not go all the way down either—or if it does, its winds at ground level are very weak. In the most powerful storms—like the one that struck Flint—the base of the thundercloud itself might appear to simply dip to the ground, and at close range the violently churning cloud may bear little resemblance to what most people expect a tornado to look like. Their disguised appearance, along with their sheer strength, makes these tornadoes the most dangerous of all. Further, if the funnel is surrounded by rain it might not be visible at all. At any rate, the classic "Wizard of Oz" elephant trunk funnels are photogenic and popular in weather books, but they're not all that common.

Just as large cyclones spawn rotating supercell thunderstorms, which in turn spin off tornadoes, tornadoes themselves can create even smaller whirls. This tendency for big whirls to make little whirls is one of the great truths of meteorology. (Ultimately, all this spinning comes from the largest whirl of them all, the earth's rotation!) The small but intense whirlwinds that travel in circular paths around the main whirl of the tornado have been named "suction spots" (because of their action on objects on the ground), and their appearance has been compared to writhing snakes. Suction spots are typically less than 30 feet across and last only seconds, but account for some of the remarkably erratic patterns of destruction observed in "multiple-vortex tornadoes." One of the spinning "fingers" in the Flint tornado slipped between a house and a barn, destroying a tree but leaving the buildings intact.

Unfortunately, the smaller and briefer a weather phenomenon is, the harder it is to predict. The problem is multiplied with tornadoes because of their lethal nature. Any attempts

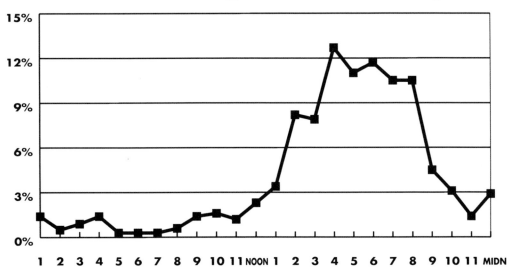

MICHIGAN TORNADOES
Percent occurring each hour of the day

Data from National Oceanographic and Atmospheric Administration © A&WGP

MICHIGAN ANNUAL NUMBER OF TORNADOES
Yearly total 1916-1992

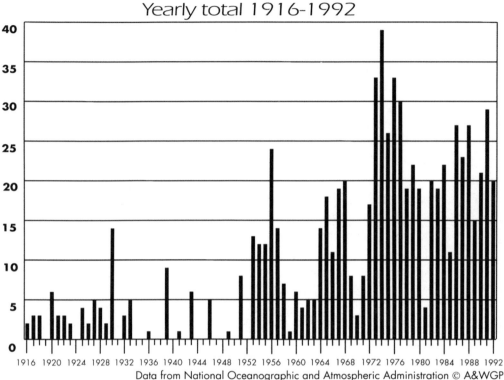

Data from National Oceanographic and Atmospheric Administration © A&WGP

to forecast these deadly storms, however, is worth the effort. In 1887, John Finley of the U.S. Army Signal Corps wrote, "Tornado prediction is no longer a mere possibility, but in many respects may be considered an accomplished fact. By this I do not mean absolute perfection, but reasonable success." Despite vast advances in our understanding of tornadoes and their causes, these words could have been written yesterday. Over the century, forecasters have improved their skills at recognizing the proper conditions—moisture, instability and so on—in which tornadoes are likely to break out. When these conditions occur, the National Weather Service issues a "Tornado Watch," stating that tornadoes are possible in an area 100 or so miles across sometime during the next few hours. Until recently, however, they couldn't issue a "Tornado Warning," meaning a twister *will* strike a certain place at a certain time, until someone had actually seen the funnel cloud or the tornado was already on the ground. A change in the 1990s will be that the latest in meteorological technology, Doppler radar, will become operational across the United States. By virtue of its ability to sense wind motions in the atmosphere, and in particular little swirls that may become tornadoes, Doppler Radar may provide up to 20 minutes advance notice of developing twisters. Twenty minutes is not a whole lot of time, considering it takes five or ten minutes to get the warning out to the public, but the remaining ten minutes is still sufficient to get a school full of kids into the basement or hallway.

Nineteen fifty-three was a terrible year for tornadoes. Just 18 days before the Flint disaster, six people died in a twister that crossed from Port Huron to Sarnia, Ontario. Two weeks earlier, another tornado had taken 114 lives at Waco, Texas. During the two hours preceding the Flint storm, killer tornadoes struck near Ypsilanti, Tawas City, and Erie, Michigan. And less than 20 hours afterwards another tornado killed 90 in Worcester, Massachusetts. If there was a silver lining to these deadly funnel clouds, it was that the rash of disasters prompted some major improvements to our systems of forecasting, detecting, and—perhaps most important—alerting the public of imminent tornadoes. The improvements have worked. Forty years and 30,000 tornadoes have passed since 1953, but there has not been another tornado as deadly as the one near Flint that awful evening in June.

SOME OUTSTANDING MICHIGAN TORNADOES

YEAR	DATE	LOCATION	DEATHS	DAMAGE/$MILLIONS
1834	2/?	Near Detroit	0	?
		Michigan's first recorded tornado		
1875	6/27	Detroit	2	?
		30 houses destroyed		
1882	4/6	Van Buren to Oakland counties	10	?
		6+ tornadoes		
1883	7/23	Eaton Rapids to Leslie	3	?
1896	5/25	Oakland & Lapeer counties	47	?
1905	6/5	Sanilac County	5	
		Wiped out 3 farms		
1917	6/6	Battle Creek to South Lyon	4	1.0
		Possibly 3 tornadoes		
1920	3/28	Southwest Lower Michigan	14	2.0
		14+ tornadoes		
1939	8/8	Kalamazoo County	2	1.1
1946	6/17	South of Detroit	0	1.0
		15 killed in Windsor, Ontario		
1953	5/21	Near Port Huron	2	2.5
		4 killed in Sarnia, Ontario		
1953	6/8	Southern Michigan	125	

Above: *A rare Upper Peninsula tornado in July 1992 cut across a field prior to striking the north side of Gladstone.*
Right: *The remains of a residential neighborhood after the devastating 1953 Flint tornado.*

COURTESY STATE ARCHIVES OF MICHIGAN

SOLID STATE

■■■■■■■■■■■■■■■■■■■■■■■■■■■■

It's hard to imagine what life would be like without ice. Without ice, what would there be to ski on? There would be nothing to shovel in the winter, and no reason to change tires twice a year. No "frost on the pumpkin," and nothing to keep boaters from sailing and freighters from plying the Great Lakes all year long. And what would beat crops to a pulp in June? For better or worse, ice is part of life in Michigan.

Ice is frozen water, or, as physics texts would say, water in its solid state: That definition seems simple enough, but ice is far from simple. Water can freeze into ice in dozens of ways and dozens of places. The resulting ice crystals can take on any of hundreds of forms. Most forms of ice are found in Michigan, at times in enormous quantities. Forty billion tons of the frozen stuff may cover the Wolverine State and cling to its shores in one winter, possibly more ice than in any other state in the "lower 48." Michigan is truly a "solid state"!

Perhaps the most familiar thing about ice crystals is their distinctive six-sided, or hexagonal, shape (salt crystals, on the other hand, are little cubes). You can see this hexagonal pattern in snowflakes, in frost on icy window panes, and—if you look close enough— anywhere else ice has formed. Water is a molecule consisting of two hydrogen atoms attached to a single, larger oxygen atom. The angle between the hydrogen atoms is 120°, the same angle as the "corners" of a hexagon. So, when water molecules bind together to form solid ice, this 120° angle appears throughout the entire mass of ice, accounting for the characteristic six-sided structure of ice crystals.

Ice can form in all sorts of places in all sorts of ways. Ice produced in the atmosphere may fall as snow or hail to the ground, or stay in the sky as ice crystal clouds. Ice can form directly on the ground or on the surfaces of lakes, streams, and ponds. The freezing of liquid water makes ice, but ice can also "sublimate" directly from individual molecules of water vapor (a gas). Ice formed by sublimation usually grows into large, well-defined crystals, while crystals in ice frozen from liquid water may be so small that the ice appears amorphous.

It may seem obvious that ice requires only two conditions: the presence of water and below freezing temperatures. However, some varieties of ice, notably frost and "black ice" on highways, can form when the air temperature is slightly above freezing but the ground has cooled by radiation to below the freezing point. Evaporation can chill wet objects below the freezing point, even though the air is warmer than freezing. That's how you can get frozen laundry on a 35° day. On the other hand, water doesn't always freeze as soon as the temperature drops to 32° (Fahrenheit). Undisturbed pure water can remain liquid at temperatures as low as -40°; this "supercooled" water is found in clouds. Outside of clouds, most water contains enough impurities and is disturbed enough (by such things as breezes rippling the surface) to freeze right at 32°. Perhaps you've heard stories about ducks landing in supercooled ponds only to have the water freeze solid around their feet. That's a great example of supercooled water in action; however, I've never seen evidence that this duck's tale has actually ever happened!

TYPES OF SNOW CRYSTALS

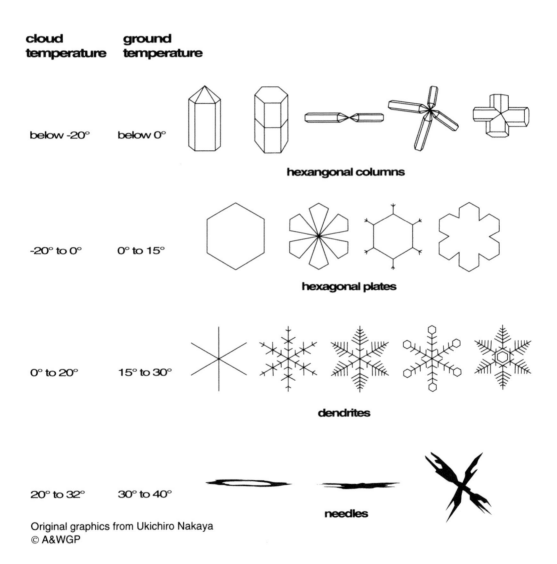

cloud temperature	ground temperature	
below -20°	below 0°	**hexangonal columns**
-20° to 0°	0° to 15°	**hexagonal plates**
0° to 20°	15° to 30°	**dendrites**
20° to 32°	30° to 40°	**needles**

Original graphics from Ukichiro Nakaya
© A&WGP

ICE FROM THE SKY

Ice forms in the sky, and falls to earth, as snow, sleet, hail, and several other varieties of frozen precipitation. Of these, the most basic and most common is snow. Virtually all of the precipitation, be it rain or frozen, that falls on Michigan initially developed as snow. Yes, even a torrential downpour on a steamy 95° August day started out as snow.

Snowflakes are born when atmospheric moisture condenses onto small particles of dust, smoke, pollen, or other airborne stuff. Most snowflakes get their moisture from supercooled water droplets in clouds, but when it's *really* cold small ice crystals grow directly from "sublimation" of water vapor, without any clouds present. Sometimes—even in the summer—snow can be seen falling from high clouds and evaporating long before reaching the ground. When the snow melts before touching down, it's called "rain"!

The structure and size of ice crystals depend on the temperature and moisture content of the air in which they form. Crystals that grow from the meager water supply at 20° below zero or colder form pencil-shaped "hexagonal columns." Around 0° to -10° most crystals are flat, six-sided "hexagonal plates." Warmer air contains more moisture, allowing larger crystals to grow. At 0° to 20° above crystals grow into large and delicate six-pointed "dendrites," from the Greek word meaning "branched like a tree." Dendrites are the largest form of snowflakes and make the fluffiest snowfalls.

Between 20° and 32° crystals grow into splinter-shaped "needles." Temperatures near the ground are typically 15 to 20 degrees higher than the temperatures at cloud height, so light, fluffy falls of dendrites are usually seen at surface temperatures in the 15° to 30° range. With all their branches, dendrites have no problem sticking to each other and creating large, multi-crystal "aggregates" as large as 2" or 3" across.

Winds above 20 m.p.h. can return fallen snow to the air, creating drifting and blowing snow. By definition, *drifting* snow remains within five feet of the snow surface, and while it does not strongly affect visibility at eye level, it can impede motor traffic by depositing snow on highways faster than plows can remove it. *Blowing* snow is raised more than five feet above the ground, which usually requires winds in excess of 35 m.p.h. A *blizzard* occurs when heavy falling snow combines with blowing snow and winds of 35 m.p.h. or higher to reduce visibility to near zero; the official weather service definition also requires temperatures of 20° or less. "Ground blizzards" of heavy blowing snow and strong winds may continue for hours or days after the falling snow has stopped. Drifts and pits of scoured and deposited wind-blown snow are known by their Russian name, "sastrugi." Strong winds may even catch the edge of a wet and sticky snow layer, rolling it up like a sleeping bag into "snow rollers"—a unique and rarely seen phenomenon.

As already mentioned, most of Michigan's rain is snow that melts while falling through above-freezing air near the ground. Sometimes from late autumn through early spring a below-freezing layer of arctic air hugs the ground while milder air streams in above (usually on the northeast side of an approaching cyclone). Then the snow that melts in the mild air refreezes before striking the ground. These refrozen rain drops are "sleet" or, officially, "ice pellets." When the cold air layer is shallower than 1,000 feet or so, the raindrops cool down but don't

51

ANNUAL AVERAGE SNOWFALL 1940-1969
(Values in inches)

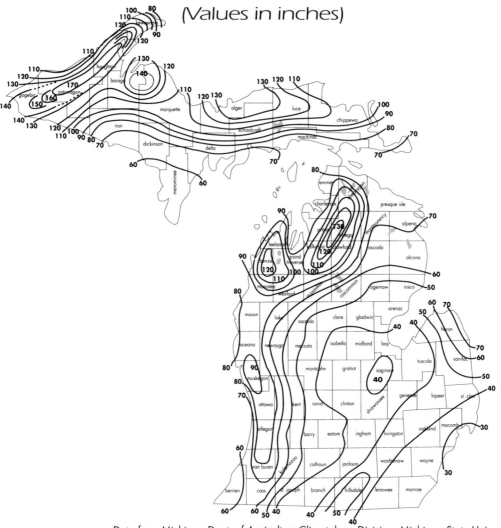

Data from Michigan Dept. of Agriculture-Climatology Division, Michigan State University
© A&WGP

freeze until they land on cold trees, roads, wires, and grass. Meteorologists call this "freezing rain" (of course!) or "glaze"; the rest of us know it as an "ice storm." While ice storms bestow the beauty of fine crystal on all they touch, the sad truth is that whatever they touch suffers a loss in value!

Another way to refreeze raindrops is send them back up to where the air is normally colder. Rain that blows back up into a storm cloud, freezes, and then falls is also sleet, and looks identical to the sleet that freezes near the ground. Before reaching the ground, a sleet pellet might catch another updraft. On its way up through the cloud it collects some additional moisture, which freezes in a layer around the original tiny pellet. Depending on its luck, the pellet may make several trips up and down in the storm cloud, growing each time. Eventually the pellet escapes the updraft, or grows so large and heavy that the wind can't keep it up, and it falls to earth as hail. Cut a hailstone open and you might see several layers of clear and white ice that were accumulated in different parts of the storm cloud, one layer for each trip through the cloud. The size of the hailstone tells something about the intensity of the storm. A baseball-size hailstone falls as fast as a major-league fastball, or about 90 m.p.h. That means updrafts of at least 90 m.p.h. lifted the stone inside the cloud. Such updrafts can easily become violent, and many large hailstorms also spawn tornadoes.

Falling ice may take other forms, such as soft, white "snow pellets" or "graupel," a cross between snow and hail; tiny "snow grains" that fall from shallow cloud layers; and "diamond dust," tiny crystals that fall from clear skies when the temperature is below zero. However, snow, rain, sleet, glaze, and hail are the main ones that fill lakes and rivers, cause traffic accidents, give skiers and snowmobilers something to do, and nourish and destroy crops.

SNOW BELTS

Nothing shows the variety of Michigan's climate more than its snowfall distribution. Statewide, Michigan averages about 70" of snow per winter, but some places get a lot more than others. In 1957, the state highway department wanted to know how much snow they had to plow from roads in the Keweenaw Peninsula, so they started measuring the white stuff at their garage in Delaware, near the tip of the peninsula. They've been busy every since—

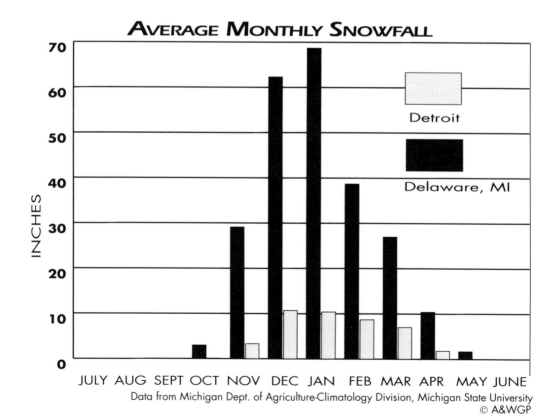

Data from Michigan Dept. of Agriculture-Climatology Division, Michigan State University
© A&WGP

50% PROBABILITY OF LAST 32° IN SPRING

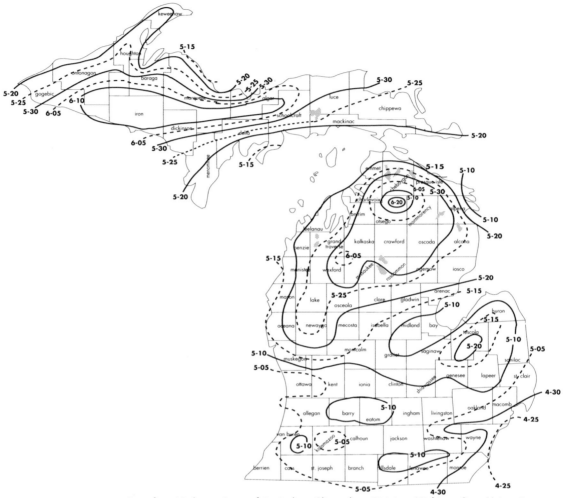

Data from Michigan Dept. of Agriculture-Climatology Division, Michigan State University
© A&WGP

in 35 years they measured 8,449 inches of snow, or over 700 feet! That's twenty feet a winter, on the average—more than eight times the meager 29" that falls on Grosse Pointe.

Away from the lakes, most of Michigan's snow falls when southeast, east, or northeast winds blow around a passing cyclone. When the storm exits the state and the winds turn to northerly and northwesterly, the snow ends for places like Detroit, Lansing, and Escanaba. At this time, however, along the eastern and southern shores of Lakes Michigan and Superior, the snow begins in earnest. Crossing the open lakes, the dry arctic air riding the northwest winds picks up moisture and then gets an upward shove as it blows ashore and up and over the inland hills. The added moisture and extra uplift provide a double whammy that creates a narrow snowbelt centered a few miles inland. Lake-effect snow squalls can be a sight to

50% PROBABILITY OF FIRST 32° IN FALL

Data from Michigan Dept. of Agriculture-Climatology Division, Michigan State University
© A&WGP

behold—they've produced snowfall rates exceeding one foot per hour, sometimes with thunder and lightning!

The hills aren't much to brag about along the southern shore of Lake Michigan; they tower no more than 400 feet above the lake. Even here, though, the snowbelt receives 60 to 100" of snow per year, twice as much as the counties to the east. The hills are higher in northern lower Michigan, reaching an elevation of 1,725 feet near Cadillac—over a thousand feet higher than Lake Michigan. Snowfall totals are also higher, and lower Michigan's snowiest place is Maple City, just west of Traverse City, where the average snowfall is 155". In another snowbelt along the 1,500-foot high plateau of northernmost lower Michigan, totals reach 145" at Gaylord. Lake- effect snows from Lake Huron brush the tip of the "Thumb," where Harbor

Beach totals 85" of snow per year. To give an idea of how much lake-effect snows add to the totals, Mt. Pleasant, which is 100 miles southeast of Maple City and away from the lake's influence, averages but 36" of snow per winter.

Along Michigan's Lake Superior shoreline, the hills are bigger (some are called mountains), the lake is larger, and the northwest winds are colder. All of these factors add up to snowier snowbelts in the U.P. than in lower Michigan. Munising averages 148" per year, but that's nothing compared to what falls in the Keweenaw Peninsula and points west. Near the tip of the Keweenaw Peninsula, the ground rises 800 feet in three miles from Lake Superior to the "spine" of the peninsula. Tremendous amounts of snow are squeezed out of the air as it ascends the steep slope, and on top of the ridge the 241" that buries Delaware in an average year makes it Michigan's snowiest place. Directly below Delaware on the lake shore, Eagle Harbor receives only 72" per year. The snowbelt extends southwest into Wisconsin, with the heaviest snow falling about 10 miles in from the lake. On the south side of the U.P. and out of range of Superior's lake-effect snows, Menominee gets only 45" of snow per year. And on the north side of Lake Superior, where the northwest winds are still dry prior to crossing the lake, Isle Royale receives 86" of snow. Perhaps as amazing as the amount of snow that lake squalls can deliver is how incredibly localized these storms can be!

Sleet is not all that common in Michigan, occurring about six to eight times a year for most locations, most frequently in lake-effect rain showers along the southeast shore of Lake Michigan. Glaze, or freezing rain, is more common, at about 12 days per year across most of the state. Detroit gets glazed about ten times a year, on the average. Fortunately, most of these are light coatings of ice. Ice gets troublesome when it accumulates .5" or more, and this happens only once every two or three years across southern lower Michigan and maybe once in five years in the northern counties. Destructive accumulations of 1" or more occur in Michigan only once every 10 or 15 years. The state's worst ice storm (1922) coated a 100-mile-wide swath with up to 2" of ice. The ice was 4" thick on wires, and the glaze on a single foot of telephone line weighed 11 pounds!

Hail, while relatively rare everywhere, is memorable. Most places in Michigan get pelted two or three times a year, on the average. A few lucky places—like Monroe, Petoskey, and Sault Ste. Marie—see hailstones only about once a year. Around Lower Michigan hail is somewhat more likely (about three times per year, mostly in September, October, and November) in the Thumb and along the shore of Lake Michigan from Manistee south. Michigan's "hail capital" lies in the U.P., where Munising averages 5 hailstorms a year. But don't let that keep you gardeners away from Munising—most of Munising's hailstones are small and soft and fall during autumn lake-effect squalls, when crops could care less about hail. More of a problem are the summer hailstorms that strike lower Michigan, where (and when) most of the state's crops are raised.

THE EIGHTH SEA

■■■■■■■■■■■■■■■■■■■■■■■■■■■■

Anyone who has never seen the Great Lakes is in for a surprise. Forget about your duck ponds and glassy sheets of water—the Great Lakes add a whole new dimension to the meaning of "lake"! Their waves roll in and break on the beach in an endless procession, often with the fury of a storm-tossed sea. The lakes even create their own weather. Clouds and fog drifting ashore from the Great Lakes are almost a daily occurrence, and frequently these inland seas generate snowstorms. When the weather clears, the blue expanse curves to the horizon and beyond—you cannot see the other shore, so, for all practical purposes, you could be standing on the shores of an ocean. Indeed, the Coast Guard refers to the Great Lakes as "The Eighth Sea"!

Unlike the oceans, which have been around forever (almost), the Great Lakes are relatively new. The lakes began forming about 2 million years ago, when the first of the ice age glaciers headed south from Canada. Like an enormous file, the slowly moving mile-deep ice grated away the ground beneath it, plucking rocks from Michigan and dropping them in Iowa and Kentucky. Over the millennia glaciers came and went, scouring out ever deeper basins in soft rock and leaving hills where the rocks were harder. When the last glacier pulled out of Michigan 11,000 years ago, its melting ice quickly filled the glacier-carved basins.

For centuries glacial ice remaining over Ontario and Quebec blocked the newly formed lakes' exit to the Atlantic. The overflow from Lakes Duluth, Chicago, Saginaw, and Whittlesey (predecessors to today's Lakes Superior, Michigan, Huron, and Erie, respectively) cut channels across Minnesota, Illinois, and Ohio as it spilled into the Gulf of Mexico. One by one the lakes started draining into the Atlantic as melting glaciers opened the St. Lawrence, St. Clair, and St. Marys rivers and the Straits of Mackinac. The levels of the lakes changed drastically as various outflow channels were, in turn, blocked by ice, free-running, and dried up. Ancient beaches can still be seen all along the shores of the Great Lakes. Most of these stranded beaches appear as level terraces sitting as high as 50' above the present lakes, although some old terraces lie 500' above Lake Superior. It was only about 4,000 years ago that the Great Lakes settled down to their present sizes, shapes, and depths (approximately).

Even though the glaciers are gone, the lakes are still changing. During the ice age the tremendous weight of the ice actually depressed the ground beneath by hundreds of feet; the land is still rebounding from the removal of the burden. The ground is rising fastest in northeastern Canada where the ice was thicker and the land depression greater—even in Michigan, Sault Ste. Marie is rising nearly a foot per century faster than Benton Harbor. This means that the lakes are still tilting, especially Lake Michigan, with its north-south orientation. Relative to the Straits of Mackinac, Chicago and Benton Harbor have sunk 8' in the past 1,000 years, and eventually Lake Michigan may regain a natural outlet at Chicago (there's already a man-made diversion of Lake Michigan into the Chicago River).

By some measures, the Great Lakes can be considered the greatest lakes on earth, while by other measures they rate second, third, and even lower. The following table compares the Great Lakes (plus Lake St. Clair) among themselves and with the world's other great fresh-water lake, Lake Baikal in Siberia. No doubt you'll want to spend a few minutes looking at and comparing the numbers for yourself, but allow me to point out a few superlatives. In terms of surface area, Lake Superior is the world's largest fresh-water lake. Even the smallest of the Great Lakes, Ontario, still ranks as the world's twelfth-largest. Although Lake Baikal has less than half the area of Lake Superior, Baikal is much deeper and holds twice as much fresh water; its volume is actually slightly more than that of all the Great Lakes combined! Russia is also the home of the salty Caspian Sea (actually an inland lake), which is five times larger than Superior (in area) and nearly twice as vast as all the Great Lakes combined. So, depending on how you choose to look at it, the Great Lakes may rank first, second, or even twelfth. But no matter how they rank, the Great Lakes are natural treasures worthy of our admiration and respect.

VITAL STATISTICS

LAKE	SUPERIOR	MICHIGAN	HURON	ONTARIO	ERIE	ST. CLAIR	BAIKAL
Length (miles):	350	307	206	193	210	26	395
Width (miles):	160	118	183	53	57	24	50
Area (square miles):	31,700	22,278	22,973	7,340	9,906	490	12,162
Shoreline (miles):	2,726	1,659	3,827	726	871	100	1,245
Elevation (feet):	602	579	579	245	571	574	1,496
Average depth (feet):	489	279	194	282	62	12	2,396
Deepest (feet):	1,335	925	748	804	210	20	5,370
Volume (cubic miles):	2,934	1180	850	393	116	1	5,518
Replacement time (years):	191	99	22	6	2.6	0.04	–
Percent freezes:	60	40	60	15	95	100	–
August water temp (F):	53	67	64	69	72	–	–
Highest water temp (F):	73	80	81	82	86	–	–

The elevation is of the surface of the lake. "Replacement time" is how long it takes for new water flowing into and onto the lake to replace old water flowing out of the lake. "Percent freezes" is the fraction of the lake surface covered by ice at the height of an average winter. The August water temperature is the average for the center of the lake, while the highest water temperature is the warmest ever measured by ships or buoys on the lake. Sources: Michigan Sea Grant College Program, National Geographic Society, National Oceanic and Atmospheric Administration, and U.S. Army Corps of Engineers.

SLOSHES AND SEICHES

If the Great Lakes look, act, and sometimes even smell like an ocean, then they must be an ocean, right? Well, sit by the shore of a Great Lake for a few hours and you notice something is missing—the lakes have no tides! The sun will rise and set, and the moon will follow; but day in and day out, waves persistently lap at the same well-marked line on the rocks and pilings. While vacationers at the ocean move their beach towels and umbrellas every hour or so to escape the advancing tide, Great Lakes beachgoers can lie all day at the same spot within inches of the water without worrying about getting wet (unless, of course, it rains).

True, the same gravitational forces that act on the oceans also act on the lakes. But despite their large appearance from shore, the lakes are much smaller than the oceans, and so are their tides. The lunar tide on Lake Michigan, for example, has a peak range of less than two inches, and is usually much less. There are, of course, exceptions—one can imagine the surprise of lakeside Chicagoans on a fair summer day in 1954, when the water suddenly rose by over 8' and, just as quickly, returned to normal. The sudden surge severely damaged docks and piers along the lake shore, and several fishermen trapped at the end of a jetty drowned.

Michigan's lake shores have seen other equally large, but fortunately less deadly, fluctuations of the Great Lakes. The Swiss recorded surges on Lakes Constance and Geneva as far back as 1549 and named these phenomena "seiches." "Seiche" sounds a bit like "slosh," and that's essentially what a seiche is. Lift up one end of a toddler's wading pool and the water runs to the other end; set it back down and the water rushes back. The water will continue to slosh back and forth for a while, and you've got a seiche in a wading pool. On lakes, it's the wind that pushes the water to one end, raising the water level at the downwind side of the lake and lowering the level of the upwind side (this is called the "set-up"). The size of the rise on the downwind shore depends on the speed, direction, and duration of the high wind, along with the length and depth (actually, the shallowness!) of the lake. Shallowest of the Great Lakes, Lake Erie is most susceptible to wind-generated set-ups. Lake Erie's east-west orientation helps, too, because some of the strongest and most persistent winds blow from the west.

An extreme set-up occurred on Lake Erie on February 16, 1967. Six hours of 30- to 50-m.p.h. winds (gusting as high as 85 m.p.h.) behind a cold front shoved several cubic miles of water from the Michigan end of the lake towards New York. Water levels rose 8' at Buffalo and dropped 7' at Monroe, a 15-foot difference. When the winds finally ceased, the piled-up water ran downhill (from Buffalo to Monroe), and eight hours later Monroe's water level stood three feet higher than Buffalo's. The sloshing continued as Monroe's water streamed back to Buffalo. Each back-and-forth round took about 12 to 15 hours, with each succeeding fluctuation growing smaller. After a couple of days the rises and falls had shrunk to less than a foot. Damage from the set-up and seiche was relatively minor, although the high winds caused all sorts of havoc. A similar storm on December 2, 1985, lifted the lake an unprecedented 12' at Buffalo, where huge waves ripped out bulkheads and retaining walls and destroyed lakeshore homes. Meanwhile, the level at Monroe dropped 8', creating a 20-foot difference across a lake that averages only 62' deep!

The other lakes suffer seiches, too. On May 5, 1952, northwest winds lifted the lake 5' at Port Huron; when the water sloshed back to Sault Ste. Marie, the Soo Locks overflowed, flooding Portage Street. One of Lake Superior's largest seiches occurred on June 30, 1968, when four sloshes, one 6' high, swamped the shores of Keweenaw Bay. Four lakes—Superior, Michigan, Huron, and Erie—all had seiches on June 16, 1946, when an enormous line of thunderstorms swept the lakes with high winds. Fluctuations of two to four feet at Marquette, Sault Ste. Marie, and Port Huron lasted as long as 24 hours. Set-ups and seiches look a bit different when the high winds come with thunderstorms and squall lines that may last only an hour or less. Instead of generating a massive set-up that tilts the surface of the entire lake, the brief but strong gusts of a squall line push lake water ahead in a wave only a few inches high. The squall has to move pretty fast, at least 50 or 60 m.p.h., for the wave to develop, otherwise the wave keeps outrunning the squall and hasn't a chance to build up. Like a little tsunami (or "tidal wave"), the wave grows to a seiche about a foot high in shallow waters near shore, and even higher if it pushes into a bay. As the squall moves inland, its seiche may bounce off the shoreline and head back across the lake to play tricks with the water level on the other side.

Squall lines are especially common over southern Lake Michigan, where they may do a most unusual thing. The wave bouncing off the curved shoreline south of Muskegon is even more curved; as it heads back towards Wisconsin or Illinois, the wave shrinks in length and grows in height, converging on a point near the western shore. In effect the wave is *focused*, just like sunlight from one of those pocket campfire-lighter mirrors or like starlight from the big mirror in the telescope on Mt. Palomar. Depending on the direction of movement of the original squall line, the focus of the wave falls somewhere between Chicago and Milwaukee. On that fair summer day in 1954 (June 26, to be exact) when the water rose 8' and surprised those Chicagoans, the seiche had *focused* on Montrose Harbor.

FREEZE AND THAW

Michigan has a lot of ice. In an average winter some 60 or 70 cubic miles of snow descends on the Wolverine State, an amount that translates to 7 cubic miles of pure, solid ice. Add to that the 2 or 3 cubic miles of lake water that freezes along Michigan's shoreline, and you get a total of 10 cubic miles of ice in the state of Michigan at the height of winter. Some winters Michigan probably holds more ice than any other state in the Union (except, of course, Alaska). We've already looked at where the snow comes from, so let's take a peek at lake ice. There's more to this than meets the eye at first—because of some of water's unusual properties, the freezing of a lake is not just a bigger version of an ice cube tray in a freezer.

Water is strange stuff. First of all, water is one of very few substances that are liquid at what we consider "normal" temperatures and atmospheric pressures. Furthermore, water happens to solidify (freeze) at a commonly occurring temperature—unlike mercury, which freezes at -40° Fahrenheit, or iron, which "freezes" at 2,786°.

So, without suffering too much, we get to see water in both its liquid and solid state . Even stranger, though, is what water does when it freezes—it *expands*, unlike most substances, which shrink when they solidify. One pound of ice takes up 10 percent more volume than one pound of liquid water, so 10 gallons of water make 11 gallons of ice. That explains the bulges that grow in the middle of ice cubes. Looking at it another way, one gallon of water weighs about 8 pounds, but one gallon of ice weighs 10 percent *less*, or just over 7 pounds. That's why ice cubes float in water. The third and final odd property of water is what happens to it at temperatures just above freezing. Almost every known material expands when it is heated, and contracts when cooled. Water is fairly normal in that regard most of the time; as a cup of liquid water cools from its boiling point of 212°, it shrinks and becomes denser (same volume weighs more). It keeps shrinking all the way down to 39°, but then further cooling actually causes the cup of water to expand a little. This means that 39° water is denser than water at any other temperature (higher or lower), and that water at any other temperature will "float" in a layer on top of the 39° water.

The fact that water is a liquid is clearly significant for Earth's living things. The other two properties of water—that ice floats and that 33° water is "lighter" than 39° water—may seem like mere curiosities. But, if water were more "normal," and ice didn't float, and 33° water wasn't "lighter" than 39° water, Michigan's lakes—and weather—would be very, very different. Let me explain....

We'll start in the fall, when increasingly chilly air removes the summer warmth from the surface of a medium-size lake (say, Houghton Lake). The air also removes moisture from the lake (by evaporation). If the lake is still warm enough, and the air cool enough, you can see this moisture rising from the lake as streamers of steam. The cooling effect is first felt at the lake surface—autumn breezes remove heat directly from water molecules, leaving a very thin layer at the top of, say, a 50° lake chilled to 49°. As the surface layer becomes denser (or "heavier") than the rest of the lake, it sinks in little downward plumes, eventually mixing with the rest of the lake, and the whole lake cools a fraction of a degree.

By early November the whole lake has cooled to 39°. But when the surface layer cools further—to 38°—it is no longer denser than the deeper water, and it floats on top instead of sinking. The more it cools the "lighter" it gets. By late November the top layer of the lake is 32°, but still liquid, while the deeper lake water remains at 39°. The depth of the cold surface layer depends on how much it is churned by wind and waves, and big lakes (like Superior) with big waves have deeper layers than do small lakes and ponds. Shortly after the top of the lake reaches 32°, the first ice forms. Only the lake's surface layer (and not the entire depth of the lake) has cooled below 39°, so thanks to one of the peculiar properties of water, the first ice freezes several weeks sooner than it would otherwise.

On ponds, the first ice forms in clear, smooth, glass-like sheets that grow out from rocks and reeds. As the ice crystals reach out toward the center of the lake, additional ice freezes to the bottom of the glassy sheet. Tiny bubbles of trapped air give the thickening ice a milky white appearance. The ice becomes safe for walking and ice skating when it's 4" thick, and cars can be driven on clear, solid ice that's at least 8" thick.

Waves on larger lakes break up the first ice into a slushy surface layer of floating crystals, sometimes called "grease" or "frazil" ice. These crystals stick together and grow into small floes of "pancake ice." If the weather stays cold long enough, the floes freeze together into a solid sheet of "pack ice," which may eventually cover the entire lake or stay confined to near-shore areas. Wind and currents can push pieces of pack ice apart, opening up large cracks or "leads," which may close up again as the wind changes direction. When pack ice is pushed against the shore or other chunks of pack ice, the frozen layer can buckle and crumble into jagged "pressure ridges," the curse of Arctic explorers but fun to look at.

Because of their enormous volume, the Great Lakes usually don't develop substantial ice cover until late January (although bays and inlets may freeze in November). And unlike Michigan's smaller "inland" lakes, the Great Lakes rarely freeze over completely. In an average winter, on Lakes Superior, Michigan, and Huron, about half of the surface remains ice-free (mostly near the middle of the lakes), with ice packs either sticking to shore or wandering about with the changing winds. With open water in mid-winter, spray may coat ships and shoreline structures with massive loads of ice during bouts of cold and windy weather, while along the shore massive walls of ice, grounded to the beach, are built up by continuous rains of freezing spray. Paradoxically, the only one of the Great Lakes that routinely freezes over is the southernmost (but shallowest), Lake Erie. Only five percent of Lake Erie remains open in an average winter.

At long last, spring arrives. Warm winds and increasing sunshine heat the top of the ice while the relative warmth of the underlying 39° water works its way up, and the ice thins from both sides. Lake Erie's ice usually starts breaking up around the end of February, while the thaw reaches Lakes Michigan and Huron by late March. Lake Superior waits until the first of April, on average, to start losing its ice, but the enormous mass of ice that accumulated during the winter often doesn't disappear until May, and has on occasion (as in 1972) lingered into June or (as in 1876) July.

With the ice gone, summer approaching, and the sun riding higher in the sky, lake surfaces warm rapidly. When the surface temperature reaches 39°, the surface water has the same density as the deep water. After being confined to the deeper reaches since fall, the 39° bottom water is finally able to rise to the surface—bringing with it all sorts of goodies, like dead fish, that have sat on the bottom for six months. In return, oxygen-rich surface water sinks to the bottom. This turn-over period can be a smelly time, but it doesn't last long. Once the surface warms above 40° it is once again "lighter" than the deeper water.

The warming continues until late July or early August, by which time the lowering sun angle becomes ineffective at heating the lake any further. Peak water temperatures depend on the location and the size of the lake. Small lakes in southern Michigan may reach 80° in mid-summer, about the same temperature as the Pacific Ocean around Hawaii. Lake Erie's water was once measured at 86°, which, if the lake were larger, would be warm enough to breed hurricanes! On the other hand, Lake Superior normally gets no warmer than 53°, and usually not until late August, though bays and nearshore waters may get a bit warmer.

In all lakes, the surface warms more than the deep water. On a still summer day the warm

Michigan Land & Lake Temperatures
Average for each month

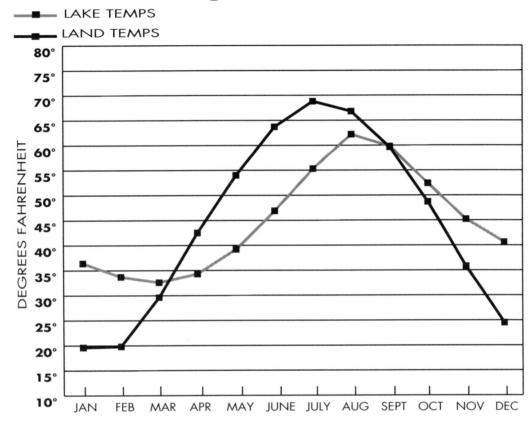

LAKE TEMPS
LAND TEMPS

Data from National Climate Data Center
© A&WGP

surface layer may be only one or two feet deep, something that does not go unnoticed by swimmers. Sunlight penetrates 100' or so into clear water, so most lakes' deep water warms up during the summer, although it never gets quite as warm as the surface. The Great Lakes are, of course, exceptions. Superior is the deepest of the Great Lakes, with most of the lake deeper than 300' and as deep as 1,290' deep at one point. At these depths the water never knows summer has come or gone, and the temperature remains 39° year-round. By September all the lakes have started cooling down for another icy winter.

Now, just for the fun of it, consider what would happen if ice did *not* float. As soon as it formed, ice would sink to bottom of rivers, lakes, and oceans. Ice, and snow lying on top of it, are great heat insulators, that is, they block the transfer of heat from one side to the other. Once lakes freeze over and the ice thickens, the rate of new ice formation slows down considerably. Without the insulating effect of floating ice sheets, surface waters continue to rapidly lose heat and the ice continue to form (and sink). Eventually, large bodies of water such as the Arctic Ocean and Hudson's Bay, and perhaps even some of the Great Lakes, might freeze solid as ice accumulated from the bottom up. Since sunlight heats only the uppermost 100' (and the topmost few feet most effectively), summer thaws would be confined to thin surface layers that would quickly refreeze the following winter. Smaller and shallower lakes would still thaw completely every summer, although it might take until June or July. Lake Superior might never thaw out! Surrounding Michigan with ice all year would have a tremendous chilling effect on the state's climate, particularly during the summer. This is all speculation, because, fortunately, ice does float.

PHOTOS COURTESY STATE ARCHIVES OF MICHIGAN

Above: *The effect of high waves combined with high lake levels on Lake Michigan. This type of shoreline erosion became a serious concern in the early 1980s.*

Right: *Before the bridge was built in 1957, entire trains were ferried across the Straits of Mackinac. An occasional railroad ferry was stuck in an ice jam.*

Above: *High winds and heavy snow, both frequent visitors to the Upper Peninsula in winter, sculpted this snowdrift near Marquette.*
Left: *This unique roadside sign along Highway 41 near Mohawk on the Keewenaw Peninsula marks the snowiest place in Michigan.*

Below: *Gale force winds and subfreezing temperatures combined to cover this lakeshore cottage near Marquette with frozen spray from Lake Superior.*
Right: *Freezing rain on New Year's Day 1985 coated a 50-mile-wide swath across the middle of Lower Michigan with an inch of glaze ice.*

TOM BUCHKOE

Above: *An ice cliff on the shore of Lake Michigan, built up over the winter from the frozen spray of breaking waves, is surrounded by small floes of pancake ice.*

Facing page, top: *Freezing spray from Lake Superior creates fantastic shapes on the lines and superstructure of a freighter. While beautiful, these ice formations create hazards for the crew, and extreme ice loads have been known to capsize ships.*
Bottom: *The Coast Guard buoy tender Mesquite, which ran aground in the fall of 1989 near Keweenaw Point, is pictured in March 1990, surrounded by pancake ice broken by wave action.*

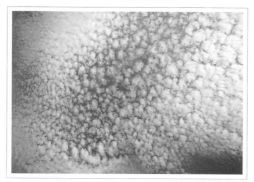

Top left: *Despite its turbulent-looking base, this layer of stratus clouds over Lake Michigan is actually quite tranquil. Rain or snow from these clouds is usually light.*

Top right: *The setting sun illuminates a layer of mammatus clouds, pouch-like formations that form beneath the high-level "anvil" cloud left by a departing thunderstorm.*

Bottom left: *Puffy cirrocumulus clouds are similar to the more familiar cumulus clouds that dot the sky on summer days, but they are much higher—6 to 8 miles up—and composed mostly of ice crystals.*

Bottom right: *Like dough rolled between your hands, cirrocumulus clouds roll into parallel bands if the wind speed is higher at the top of the cloud layer than it is at the bottom.*

Above: *Fog, which essentially is a stratus cloud that forms at ground level, rolls over Houghton from Lakes Superior.*

Persistent breezes blowing inland from the cool water of Lake Michigan left these ripples in the sand at Sleeping Bear Dune.

Like billions of tiny mirrors, flat ice crystals falling slowly through the air reflect the light of the setting sun into vertical "sun pillars."

Facing page, top: *Sunlight shining through a broken cloud layer over the Straits of Mackinac create "crepuscular rays," known years ago as "sun drawing water" in the mistaken impression that the rays were rising shafts of water vapor.*
Bottom: *Light rain falls from a layer of stratocumulus clouds, a common cloud type over Michigan—especially after the passage of a cold front.*

*Lightning rakes Beaver Island
during a summer storm.*

Above: *After the the June 1989 tornado at Park Lake.* **Right:** *July 1988 storm damage near Marquette.*

Alternating white and clear layers in hailstones that fell on Sault Ste. Marie in March 1989 tell the story of the stones' growth as they traveled up and down between the warmer and colder regions of the thunderstorm.

Ice crystals.

Left: *The red light of the setting sun mutes the blues and greens in this double rainbow. Note, however, that the order of colors is reversed between the inner and outer bows.*

Refraction by the atmosphere distorts the image of the setting sun until, at last, the elusive green flash appears at the last moment. The dark specks on the sun are sunspots.

LOCAL CLIMATE DATA

■■■■■■■■■■■■■■■■■■■■■■■■■■■■

The National Weather Service operates nine full-time weather stations in the state of Michigan—only Alaska, California, Florida, and Texas can brag of more. These nine stations, however, can only hint at the true variety of Michigan's many climates. Fortunately, dozens of other weather stations are located at small airports, hospitals, dams, parks, forest range stations, mines, fisheries, colleges, lighthouses, power plants, radio stations, and even sewage treatment facilities. Even more weather stations are operated by interested families and individuals, many living on farms. An outstanding example of these dedicated weather watchers was Mr. Albert Oas, who checked the thermometer and measured the snow at Munising just about every day from 1911 until 1959. We owe these volunteers an enormous debt for their long-term efforts, without which our knowledge of Michigan's climate would be much less complete. Perhaps this may inspire you to set up your own weather station— after five or ten years, you'll have a pretty good idea how your average temperature, rainfall, and snowfall compares with the nearest "official" station.

Not every lighthouse and sewage plant in Michigan has its own weather station, but here's a list of climate data for most of those places that do (or did at some time in the past). The numbers come from a variety of sources, including the National Climate Data Center in Asheville, North Carolina, and the Michigan State Climatologist's office in East Lansing. Some locations are major (or minor) urban centers, in or near which many readers might live. In some towns weather records are kept at the airport. For the benefit of sailors and boaters, I've thrown in some approximate climate statistics for the open waters of Lakes Superior, Michigan, Huron, and Erie. These data are based on shipboard weather observations combined with records from floating automated weather stations operated by the National Data Buoy Center.

Modern weather stations can produce a bewildering variety of data. The more relevant and interesting statistics include:

Elevation (feet)—Normally, the climate cools by 1° for every 200 or 300 feet of elevation gain, a rule of thumb that works pretty well during the winter. In summer, however, the lakes' cooling influences overwhelm any effects of elevation, and many of Michigan's high spots— being relatively far from the nearest lake—are warmer than lower lakeshore locations.

Year Records Begin—The longer weather records have been taken, the more reliable the averages will be. It takes about 10 or 20 years to come up with a truly representative average. For comparing one place with another, it's best to compute averages over the same period of years. Most, but not all, of the averages listed here are for the most recent "official" averaging period, 1951 through 1980. Some weather stations closed down before 1980 or opened up after 1951, in which cases some other averaging period (obviously) had to be chosen.

Average Temperature (Fahrenheit)—Annual average temperatures are fairly worthless at describing a place's climate—Detroit's 49° annual average is closely matched by London, England (50°); Seoul, Korea (52°); La Paz, Bolivia (50°); Cuzco, Peru (52°); Beijing, China (53°); Reno, Nevada (49°); Mount Shasta, California (50°), and Mount Haleakala, Hawaii (48°). None of these places has summers or winters quite like those found in Michigan, even though the averages are the same. Average daily high and low temperatures for July and January, listed here, give a much better picture of the daily and seasonal ranges of temperature.

Temperature Extremes—These are the highest and lowest temperatures since records began. The more years of record, the more extreme the extremes are likely to be. In particular, most of Michigan's all-time high temperatures were set in July 1936, and weather stations not in operation that summer are likely to show lower record high temperatures than other nearby locations.

Last/First Freezing Temperature in Spring/Fall—The average dates of the last and first 32° overnight minimum temperatures give an idea of when tender plants can be planted and when they need to be harvested or brought inside. In half the years, the actual first or last freeze occurs within 10 days of the average date, but in extreme years the freeze can be up to three or four weeks "off schedule." Being below the ground, many seeds can be planted before the last spring freeze, while root vegetables and other hardy plants may keep growing past the first autumn freeze.

Average Annual Precipitation (inches)—Precipitation includes the water contained in snow, hail, sleet, etc., as well as rain. As a rule, 10" of snow melts down to 1" of precipitation.

Average Annual Snowfall (inches)—The total of all the individual storms in a year.

MICHIGAN LOCAL CLIMATE DATA

LOWER PENINSULA

STATION	ELEV.	YEAR RECORDS BEGIN	AVERAGE TEMP. JULY MAX.	MIN.	JAN. MAX.	MIN.	TEMP. EXTREMES HIGH	LOW	LAST/FIRST FREEZING TEMP SPRING	FALL	AVERAGE ANNUAL PRECIP.	SNOW
Adrian	754	1887	84	60	31	15	108	-26	May 3	Oct 6	32.81	32.3
Allegan	629	1886	84	60	31	16	106	-29	May 8	Oct 6	35.71	79.7
Alma	740	1887	84	59	29	14	108	-29	May 8	Oct 7	29.55	41.8
Alpena (city)	586	1872	77	58	27	13	104	-28	May 9	Oct 12	27.60	67.3
Alpena Airport	689	1959	80	53	27	9	102	-37	May 26	Sep 21	28.92	85.9
Ann Arbor	871	1880	84	62	31	17	105	-23	Apr 29	Oct 20	30.32	35.7
Atlanta	880	1927	81	54	28	9	104	-46	Jun 2	Sep 16	27.68	65.9
Bad Axe	715	1925	81	57	28	13	103	-23	May 13	Oct 5	29.33	54.3
Baldwin	825	1938	83	55	29	11	104	-49	May 29	Sep 17	33.97	82.7
Battle Creek Airport	934	1876	83	60	30	15	105	-24	May 5	Oct 7	33.90	48.9
Bay City	590	1896	82	61	29	15	110	-31	May 1	Oct 17	27.92	38.7
Benton Harbor Airport	649	1878	82	61	31	18	104	-21	May 5	Oct 14	36.51	70.3
Big Rapids	930	1887	82	56	28	11	103	-36	May 20	Sep 25	31.90	70.5
Bloomingdale	725	1904	83	59	30	16	105	-22	May 10	Oct 8	38.25	90.7
Boyne Falls	830	1960	82	55	27	11	102	-35	Jun 5	Sep 11	33.23	130.3
Cadillac	1295	1898	79	54	25	10	104	-43	Jun 3	Sep 12	30.81	71.2
Caro	670	1928	84	57	29	13	108	-30	May 23	Sep 23	28.23	36.5
Charlotte	897	1902	84	57	30	12	106	-31	May 15	Sep 26	32.95	47.6
Cheboygan	586	1890	79	57	27	11	104	-38	May 16	Oct 12	27.99	77.9
Coldwater	984	1887	82	59	30	15	108	-23	May 6	Oct 3	33.49	47.8
Dearborn	601	1954	85	62	32	17	104	-17	Apr 26	Oct 16	30.89	30.7
Detroit City Airport	619	1818	83	64	31	19	105	-24	Apr 22	Oct 24	29.82	35.2
Detroit Metro Airport	633	1897	84	60	31	16	107	-24	May 1	Oct 15	31.65	41.1
Dowagiac	735	1939	84	59	31	15	103	-23	May 12	Oct 3	37.36	73.1
East Jordan	590	1926	80	55	28	13	103	-41	May 31	Sep 21	31.78	93.3
East Lansing MSU	888	1863	82	59	29	13	102	-37	May 8	Oct 4	28.67	38.7
East Tawas	590	1887	80	56	29	11	106	-29	May 20	Sep 29	29.46	49.5
Eau Claire	870	1924	83	62	30	17	107	-21	May 1	Oct 19	35.12	69.9
Evart	1025	1941	82	54	27	9	100	-30	May 28	Sep 13	30.56	53.2
Fife Lake	1080	1919	80	53	26	9	107	-45	Jun 5	Sep 13	31.34	105.1
Flint Airport	771	1888	81	59	29	14	108	-28	May 9	Oct 9	29.29	45.2
Frankfort/Elberta	589	1906	77	58	27	16	99	-32	May 25	Oct 6	30.40	97.3
Gaylord	1349	1887	80	55	25	10	101	-39	May 28	Sep 17	33.59	145.3
Gladwin	770	1928	82	56	28	10	105	-39	May 18	Sep 22	31.48	51.6
Grand Haven	622	1871	79	62	31	19	101	-25	Apr 28	Oct 18	31.28	75.0
Grand Rapids Airport	784	1849	83	60	29	15	108	-24	May 6	Oct 8	33.73	72.3
Grayling	1140	1899	81	54	26	9	106	-42	May 30	Sep 17	31.95	92.9
Greenville	882	1912	84	58	29	14	108	-25	May 12	Sep 30	33.06	55.4
Grosse Pointe	581	1947	84	63	32	18	105	-16	Apr 27	Oct 22	31.64	28.7
Gull Lake	890	1929	84	60	30	15	108	-21	May 7	Oct 7	34.00	58.5

STATION	ELEV.	YEAR RECORDS BEGIN	AVERAGE TEMP. JULY MAX.	MIN.	JAN. MAX.	MIN.	TEMP. EXTREMES HIGH	LOW	LAST/FIRST FREEZING TEMP SPRING	FALL	AVERAGE ANNUAL PRECIP.	SNOW
Hale	800	1913	80	55	27	8	107	-40	May 20	Sep 28	28.05	50.8
Harbor Beach	620	1887	78	59	28	15	105	-24	May 8	Oct 16	34.27	85.4
Harrisville	675	1888	78	55	29	13	107	-30	May 20	Oct 5	28.78	61.2
Hart	675	1887	81	58	29	16	104	-35	May 15	Oct 5	34.34	98.8
Hastings	730	1887	84	59	30	15	109	-31	May 13	Sep 29	31.22	51.9
Hesperia	770	1938	82	56	29	13	100	-35	May 26	Sep 25	33.57	75.5
Higgins Lake	1190	1888	81	54	26	8	106	-39	May 29	Sep 19	32.35	73.8
Hillsdale	1100	1889	82	58	30	15	107	-21	May 13	Sep 27	37.75	56.7
Holland	678	1905	82	60	31	18	105	-43	May 7	Oct 10	35.68	96.0
Houghton Lake Airport	1149	1912	79	55	25	9	107	-48	May 28	Sep 17	27.99	75.8
Ionia	850	1889	84	58	30	14	103	-25	May 13	Sep 28	31.53	44.4
Jackson Airport	998	1897	83	61	29	15	105	-21	May 7	Oct 7	29.11	38.6
Kalamazoo	945	1865	85	61	31	17	109	-25	May 1	Oct 13	34.83	73.1
Lake City	1230	1892	81	54	26	9	106	-41	May 29	Sep 15	28.86	78.1
Lansing Airport	841	1930	83	59	29	14	102	-29	May 10	Oct 2	29.57	48.6
Lapeer	865	1896	83	58	29	13	105	-26	May 16	Sep 24	27.91	47.5
Ludington	662	1896	80	58	29	16	99	-38	May 18	Oct 4	31.86	82.8
Lupton	890	1951	82	51	27	6	102	-34	Jun 10	Sep 5	29.26	57.2
Mackinaw City	588	1896	77	57	26	11	104	-33	May 15	Oct 17	30.40	77.5
Manistee	585	1888	80	59	29	16	100	-38	May 10	Oct 16	30.92	92.0
Maple City	730	1958	81	56	27	14	99	-24	May 27	Oct 5	34.86	154.6
Midland	617	1896	83	60	29	15	106	-30	May 7	Oct 6	28.71	37.7
Milan/Willis	660	1929	83	58	30	14	105	-23	May 11	Sep 25	31.28	38.6
Milford	1188	1928	81	60	28	14	104	-20	May 6	Oct 11	31.58	45.3
Mio	963	1888	81	54	27	8	112	-47	May 29	Sep 19	27.16	69.1
Monroe	582	1917	84	63	32	17	106	-21	Apr 23	Oct 21	30.93	32.7
Montague	650	1949	80	57	31	16	98	-35	May 23	Oct 8	33.55	89.5
Mt. Clemens Airport	577	1896	82	62	30	17	106	-24	Apr 27	Oct 19	28.18	34.3
Mt. Pleasant	796	1887	83	58	29	13	106	-30	May 11	Oct 3	30.24	36.3
Muskegon Airport	625	1896	80	60	29	17	99	-30	May 7	Oct 11	31.49	97.5
Newaygo	757	1907	83	54	30	12	111	-37	May 25	Sep 28	31.84	57.0
North Manitou Island	585	1954	76	57	29	18	96	-6	(only 6 years of record)			
Onaway State Park	690	1928	81	55	27	10	106	-35	May 19	Sep 25	30.98	89.0
Owosso	738	1896	82	59	29	14	105	-26	May 11	Oct 3	28.79	41.1
Paw Paw	705	1924	85	60	32	17	108	-24	May 10	Oct 6	36.09	74.8
Pellston Airport	710	1941	79	52	25	7	103	-37	Jun 8	Sep 6	31.84	117.5
Petoskey	660	1890	78	58	27	15	101	-35	May 10	Oct 16	30.31	100.2
Pontiac	974	1887	84	61	30	15	104	-22	May 3	Oct 13	29.30	34.8
Port Huron	586	1874	82	62	30	17	104	-25	May 1	Oct 19	30.65	41.7
Saginaw Airport	662	1896	82	60	27	14	111	-23	May 3	Oct 13	29.76	45.8
St. Charles	596	1952	85	59	29	14	101	-25	May 6	Oct 5	28.30	48.4
St. James	598	1952	76	56	26	14	97	-28	May 20	Oct 15	29.02	66.3
St. Johns	755	1887	84	59	30	14	102	-22	May 10	Oct 6	30.07	44.3
Sandusky	774	1909	82	58	29	14	103	-23	May 11	Oct 6	27.97	53.9

STATION	ELEV.	YEAR RECORDS BEGIN	AVERAGE TEMP. JULY MAX.	JULY MIN.	JAN. MAX.	JAN. MIN.	TEMP. EXTREMES HIGH	LOW	LAST/FIRST FREEZING TEMP SPRING	FALL	AVERAGE ANNUAL PRECIP.	SNOW
South Haven	626	1895	79	61	32	18	100	-22	May 2	Oct 18	35.03	60.1
Standish	616	1938	82	56	28	11	100	-26	May 19	Sep 23	27.81	45.3
Three Rivers	810	1895	84	60	31	15	107	-22	May 7	Oct 1	33.55	45.8
Traverse City Airport	618	1877	81	57	26	13	105	-37	May 24	Oct 3	29.71	86.6
Vanderbilt	925	1923	81	50	26	6	108	-51	Jun 19	Aug 22	30.47	113.8
West Branch	1064	1887	81	55	26	9	107	-36	May 22	Sep 26	28.87	57.3
Ypsilanti	779	1863	84	62	30	16	107	-25	Apr 29	Oct 16	29.76	36.2

UPPER PENINSULA

STATION	ELEV.	YEAR RECORDS BEGIN	AVERAGE TEMP. JULY MAX.	JULY MIN.	JAN. MAX.	JAN. MIN.	TEMP. EXTREMES HIGH	LOW	LAST/FIRST FREEZING TEMP SPRING	FALL	AVERAGE ANNUAL PRECIP.	SNOW
Alberta	1310	1956	78	54	20	2	100	-38	Jun 9	Sep 11	34.40	151.1
Beechwood	1660	1951	78	53	21	1	96	-36	Jun 4	Sep 16	33.55	106.0
Bergland	1300	1915	78	52	20	-1	100	-48	Jun 5	Sep 14	38.35	171.7
Calumet Airport	1081	1887	75	54	20	6	102	-35	May 17	Sep 27	34.11	203.0
Champion/Humboldt	1565	1939	78	50	21	0	102	-49	Jun 15	Aug 25	33.65	138.0
Chatham	875	1900	78	52	24	7	103	-44	Jun 13	Sep 13	34.80	146.1
Delaware	1200	1957	(No temperature records taken)									241.5
De Tour	585	1900	74	56	23	7	102	-39	May 12	Oct 13	29.75	68.0
Dunbar Forest	600	1942	76	52	23	5	98	-39	May 27	Sep 28	31.94	99.0
Eagle Harbor	626	1902	73	54	25	13	100	-26	May 23	Oct 13	29.12	72.3
Escanaba	594	1871	75	58	24	9	100	-32	May 8	Oct 8	28.26	49.9
Ewen	1147	1904	78	51	21	1	101	-49	Jun 10	Sep 13	29.10	111.7
Fayette/Sack Bay	788	1920	75	57	25	10	96	-28	May 12	Oct 8	29.87	60.3
Grand Marais	755	1919	75	51	24	11	99	-32	Jun 11	Sep 22	31.34	143.2
Houghton	668	1901	75	55	22	7	104	-31	May 15	Oct 11	32.50	115.7
Iron Mountain	1155	1899	80	55	23	3	104	-39	May 28	Sep 17	30.36	63.3
Ironwood	1520	1901	79	55	20	1	104	-41	May 28	Sep 17	34.90	155.5
Ishpeming	1436	1898	78	54	22	5	102	-34	May 31	Sep 17	31.87	118.5
Isle Royale												
Mott Island	620	1941	69	50	19	6	94	-29	May 22	Oct 3	29.38	86.3
Rock of Ages	603	1983	—	—	—	—	85	-18				
Passage Island	642	1984	—	—	—	—	74	-18				
Kenton	1167	1940	80	51	22	1	100	-46	Jun 17	Aug 30	30.31	104.6
Mackinac Island	831	1901	75	55	25	10	99	-27	May 19	Oct 10	30.81	77.3
Manistique	610	1896	76	54	26	8	101	-36	May 26	Sep 19	31.72	70.7
Marquette (city)	677	1857	75	57	24	11	108	-27	May 13	Oct 18	30.81	112.2
Marquette Airport	1415	1979	76	53	19	2	99	-34	Jun 3	Sep 16	34.64	127.0
Menominee/Marinette	598	1899	84	59	27	-9	108	-30	May 11	Oct 5	32.01	45.4
Munising	640	1896	76	53	25	9	103	-40	Jun 6	Sep 21	33.45	148.1
Newberry	886	1896	76	53	23	8	103	-32	May 27	Sep 25	32.94	108.3
Ontonagon	701	1900	78	54	24	8	102	-42	Jun 2	Sep 20	30.67	117.5
Rudyard	750	1951	76	53	21	6	99	-34	May 30	Sep 22	34.13	115.3

STATION	ELEV.	YEAR RECORDS BEGIN	AVERAGE TEMP. JULY MAX.	AVERAGE TEMP. JULY MIN.	AVERAGE TEMP. JAN. MAX.	AVERAGE TEMP. JAN. MIN.	TEMP. EXTREMES HIGH	TEMP. EXTREMES LOW	LAST/FIRST FREEZING TEMP SPRING	LAST/FIRST FREEZING TEMP FALL	AVERAGE ANNUAL PRECIP.	AVERAGE ANNUAL SNOW
St. Ignace	593	1889	77	52	26	10	99	-35	May 19	Oct 4	26.88	57.8
Sault Ste Marie Airport	721	1888	75	52	21	5	98	-37	May 25	Sep 27	33.48	116.5
Seney/Germfask	710	1939	79	53	25	7	103	-47	May 26	Sep 25	33.12	131.5
Stambaugh	1485	1902	79	52	22	1	103	-47	Jun 7	Aug 29	31.82	77.5
Stannard Rock	602	1984	—	—	—	—	87	-12				
Stephenson	715	1949	81	54	24	4	101	-39	May 30	Sep 18	32.63	65.2
Watersmeet	1630	1909	79	52	21	1	100	-47	Jun 13	Aug 28	33.61	113.6
Whitefish Point	610	1900	71	51	24	11	100	-30	May 30	Oct 4	33.51	129.9

ON THE LAKES (*)

STATION	ELEV.	YEAR RECORDS BEGIN	JULY MAX.	JULY MIN.	JAN. MAX.	JAN. MIN.	HIGH	LOW
Superior (western)	602	1981	58	53	25	23	88	-8
Superior (northern)	602	1979	55	51	27	25	84	-12
Superior (eastern)	602	1980	56	51	28	26	90	-8
Michigan (northern)	579	1979	67	61	25	23	90	-8
Michigan (southern)	579	1981	69	65	26	24	91	-8
Huron (northern	579	1980	67	61	31	29	90	7
Huron (southern)	579	1981	68	64	33	32	97	5
Erie (western)	571	1980	74	70	37	36	92	14

* The extreme lows for the lakes are the lowest temperatures reported by ships and buoys on the Great Lakes. Lower temperatures have undoubtedly occurred when the lake was frozen, but, of course, there were no ships or buoys out to record it (weather buoys are brought ashore for the winter). Except for Lake Michigan, December temperatures appear in the January "Max" and "Min" columns, due to the scarcity of shipboard readings in January.

For those weather stations that record these things, here are some additional statistics of interest:

Number of Thunderstorms—Actually, the average yearly number of days with thunderstorms. Some days may have two or more thunderstorms, but this doesn't affect the average.

Number of Clear and Cloudy Days—On a clear day, clouds cover three tenths or less of the sky, on the average, from sunrise to sunset. This could mean solid overcast for three hours, then completely clear for the rest of the day, or it could mean scattered puffy clouds all day long. A cloudy day is one on which eight tenths or more of the sky is covered, on average, between sunup and sundown.

Percent Sunshine—This is the percentage of possible sunshine—the monthly number of hours that the sun shines, given as a percentage of the number of hours the sun would have shone had the skies been clear all month. December is Michigan's cloudiest month, and July is the sunniest.

1 P.M. Humidity—Average relative humidity, in percent, at 1 P.M. Eastern Standard Time (EST) in January and July.

Fog—Number of days per year with fog reducing visibility to one-quarter mile or less.

LOWER PENINSULA

STATION	NO. OF THUNDER-STORMS	NO. OF DAYS CLEAR	NO. OF DAYS CLOUDY	PERCENT SUNSHINE DEC.	PERCENT SUNSHINE JULY	1 PM HUMIDITY JAN.	1 PM HUMIDITY JULY	DAYS/W HEAVY FOG
Alpena Airport	34	67	193	27	67	70	53	26
Detroit (downtown)	29	—	—	29	68	76	53	11
Detroit City Airport	32	80	177	32	70	69	51	11
Detroit Metro Airport	33	77	183	29	69	69	53	22
Flint Airport	33	66	194	—	—	71	55	18
Grand Haven	30	—	—	21	73	80	64	12
Grand Rapids Airport	37	65	204	21	64	72	55	27
Houghton Lake Airport	39	65	199	—	—	72	54	30
Lansing Airport	34	72	189	28	70	75	56	23
Ludington	37	—	—	20	76	82	71	11
Muskegon Airport	38	77	200	—	—	75	59	25
Port Huron	—	—	—	28	68	78	58	—

UPPER PENINSULA

STATION	NO. OF THUNDER-STORMS	NO. OF DAYS CLEAR	NO. OF DAYS CLOUDY	PERCENT SUNSHINE DEC.	PERCENT SUNSHINE JULY	1 PM HUMIDITY JAN.	1 PM HUMIDITY JULY	DAYS/W HEAVY FOG
Escanaba	33	102	155	34	66	70	65	19
Houghton	23	—	—	16	61	79	64	16
Marquette (city)	29	61	203	28	67	68	63	17
Marquette Airport	—	—	—	25	64	—	—	—
Sault Ste Marie Airport	30	66	208	27	63	75	61	46

The USAF Defense Meteorological Satellite Program (DMSP) gives us this view of the Great Lakes region from space, by the light of the full moon.

MICHIGAN BY MOONLIGHT

■■■■■■■■■■■■■■■■■■■■■■■■■■■■

With its lakes, forests, hills, and farms, Michigan is a beautiful place to explore by land, lake, and even from the air. But here's a truly unique perspective of the Wolverine State— a night view from space! This image was taken by an Air Force weather satellite at 10:58 P.M. on December 30, 1990, by the light of the full moon.

Despite the late hour, moonlight reflecting from snow-covered ground contrasts with the dark water of the unfrozen Great Lakes, and the "mitten" of lower Michigan is clearly visible. At the time of the picture, the entire state was under cold northwesterly winds with temperatures ranging from around 20° in the southeast to near 0° across the Upper Peninsula. The weather pattern was ideal for lake-effect snows; flurries dusted the southern and eastern shores of Lakes Superior, Michigan, Huron, Erie, and St. Clair. Streamers of snow-bearing clouds aligned with the northwesterly winds to form some remarkably complex patterns— it's easy to see why lake-effect snows can be so locally variable. This picture also clearly and remarkably reproduces the lights of Michigan's cities and towns. Metropolitan Detroit appears as a big bright spot, with lesser spots to the north and west marking Flint, Lansing, and Grand Rapids. Chicago and Milwaukee grace the southwestern fringe of Lake Michigan, while St. Ignace and Mackinaw City appear as tiny dots separated by the Straits of Mackinac. Duluth (Minnesota) and the combined lights of the two Sault Ste. Marie's sit at opposite tips of Lake Superior. With care, patience, and a good map, you may be able to locate the towns of Baraga (population 1,231), Beaverton (1,150), Stephenson (904), Tekonsha (752), Rose City (686), and Port Sanilac (656).

City lights seen from the air—or from space—are a glorious sight that has been compared to our earthbound view of the constellations. The sad truth is that these same city lights shining up into the atmosphere actually ruin our view of the stars. It doesn't take much—most towns larger than a few thousand people have so much sky glow that it's difficult or impossible to see the Milky Way. Since the majority of the population lives in urban areas, few of us have the opportunity to look up and see what the night sky really looks like. It is a loss comparable to smoggy vistas of the Grand Canyon or the fouling of the Great Lakes, and the excess lighting of the night sky has been called "light pollution." Bright nights also hamper astronomical research and can impact the mating and migrating habits of birds and other wildlife.

Light pollution has its tangible costs as well. Light that escapes into outer space is light that is *not* illuminating streets, yards, factories, billboards, and so on—and that means wasted energy. In Michigan alone the annual price of lighting outer space is about $40 million; the national tab is about a billion dollars. The biggest offenders are streetlights that shine in all directions, including up. Fortunately, the cost can be decreased and the number of stars seen at night increased by judicious use of more efficient outdoor lighting, especially shielded fixtures that direct light *down* to their intended targets. Yes, Michigan at night is a lovely spectacle from space, but it's a spectacle that doesn't come cheaply.

THE GREEN FLASH

■■■■■■■■■■■■■■■■■■■■■■■■■■■■■

On sunny afternoons, members of the Green Flash Society climb the dunes to catch a better view of the setting sun. Just as the last of the big red ball disappears beneath the waves, a brilliant speck of green light sparkles on the horizon, and then it, too, is gone. After some "oohs" and "ahs" and brief discussions about who saw the mysterious green light and who blinked and missed it, Society members turn and descend the dunes, fulfilled and ready to face the rest of their lives.

California? Nope—it's Michigan. The dunes lining the northeastern shores of Lake Michigan provide the ideal site for watching the elusive but beautiful "green flash." Perhaps by now you're really wondering what I'm talking about. The green flash is an exceedingly brief (lasting one second or less), brilliant greenish (or, rarely, bluish) light seen on the horizon either immediately after the last of the solar disk disappears at sunset or immediately before sunrise. And, I might add, the people who look for it are quite normal—you may want to try it yourself some clear evening.

Over the years various explanations have been offered for the green flash. One of the most pervasive theories is that the green light is an after-image of the brilliant red sun that has just disappeared, much like the green blob you see after someone takes your picture with a flash camera. The green flash, however, also has been seen at sunrise—so scratch that theory. Another idea popular years ago was that the green color is the top of the sun shining through wave crests. But—alas!—the green flash is frequently seen over deserts. (Of course, none of this was a issue for the ancient Egyptians, who figured the sun turned green when it went under for the night because gods can do whatever they please!)

The *real* cause of the green flash is "refraction," the bending of rays of sunlight as they pass through the atmosphere. When the sun is near the horizon, atmospheric refraction "lifts" its image upwards by about its own diameter, giving us an extra two or three minutes of sunshine at sunset and sunrise. In addition, refraction bends blue light more than red, so at sunrise and sunset, the sun's blue and green light is lifted a little higher off the horizon than red and orange. The shifting of different colors is just enough to grace the sun's upper edge with a bluish or greenish fringe. The lower edge of the sun gets the opposite out of the deal—a reddish fringe—but it's much less obvious because the whole setting (or rising) sun is tinted red. The separation of colors is exactly the same as that of sunlight shining through a prism or crystal—in this case, the atmosphere is doing the prism's job.

It's easy to see that when the sun sets, the last light to go is the blue-green fringe on top. Unfortunately, haze and junk in the atmosphere usually dull the colors, so the sun simply disappears. But when the air is exceptionally clear (which it often is over the northern Great Lakes), that blue-green fringe can shine alone for a second or two before it vanishes; the fringe is called a "green flash" because it often appears and disappears quite suddenly. Since the atmosphere should be clear and the horizon needs to be low and flat, the best places to observe the green flash are over oceans and large lakes or from an airplane. The best time of year seems to be late summer and early fall. Don't count on seeing it every evening, though. In 33 years of looking I've only seen it nine times!

For some reason, the green flash is rarely seen at sunrise. I'm not sure why this should be—it could be related to different degrees of refraction in the cooler morning air, but that's pure speculation. Also, most people are still in bed at sunrise, and those who are up are often in a hurry to get somewhere. In other words, the green flash may be rarely seen at sunrise because it's rarely looked for!

And speaking of looking for the green flash, here are a few tips:

• Find a good spot with a clear, flat horizon—like a big dune overlooking a large lake.

• Pick a day with a deep blue, and preferably cloudless, sky. Murphy's Law says that the sun will go behind an undetected distant cloud at the last moment, but then again, it might not.

• Don't look directly at the setting sun until the moment the green flash appears. The after-image of the sun in your eyes could be mistaken for the green flash, and besides, you could damage your eyes.

• *Never* look at the sun with binoculars—you could burn millions of cells in your retina and ruin your vision forever. I've found that a good way to magnify the setting sun and green flash is to look through a camera attached to a long (500 mm) telephoto lens (stopped all the way down to its highest F-setting, like f/32 or greater). If the sun appears uncomfortably bright in the camera, wait until it sets a little lower and gets a little dimmer. Don't forget to check the sun for sunspots, and while you're at it, you might want to snap a picture.

• Even if everything else seems right for the green flash to happen, momentary fluctuations in the atmosphere's layers may or may not produce the phenomenon. Keep trying—there's no substitute for persistence and interest!

MICHIGAN'S CHANGING (?) CLIMATE

■■■■■■■■■■■■■■■■■■■■■■■■■■■■■

THE YEAR WITHOUT A SUMMER

The summer of 1992 was not your usual Michigan summer. That was obvious by the middle of August, when trees were already turning a bright red across the Upper Peninsula and yellow leaves were appearing farther south. All across the state it was the coldest summer since statewide records began in 1895, with June, July, and August averaging a whopping 4 degrees below normal. Sault Ste. Marie's July maximum was only 79°, and the summer high of 86° came in May. Sporting frost all summer, the Soo's 57.2° July average was the lowest since the Army brought thermometers to the area in 1823. And, while most summers see one or two week-long, statewide heat waves, the "dog days" never showed up in 1992. Only four days (none consecutive) had temperatures as high as 90° somewhere in the state, and then only at scattered locations in lower Michigan. With only slight exaggeration, we can say that 1992 was a "Year Without a Summer"!

Whenever odd weather strikes, people look for a cause—shifting currents in the Pacific Ocean, storms on the sun, Mideast wars, nuclear tests, hair spray, burning forests and fossil fuels, Republicans, Democrats, Communists, whatever. The truth is, though, that just as weather changes from day to day (because that's what it does for a living), the climate—measured by the warmth of a summer or the amount of snow in a winter—also changes from year to year. Climate varies because the atmosphere is not solid, and like ripples and eddies in a stream, is always in motion and never exactly repeats its past performances. This concept is called "natural variability," and it's what makes long-range weather or climate prediction next to impossible.

Having said all this, the unusual thing about the summer (or lack thereof) of '92 is that there very well may have been a cause for it. That cause could—and I emphasize *could*—be a mountain halfway around the world, a volcano—Pinatubo, in the Philippine Islands—that erupted in June 1991. After six centuries of good behavior, Pinatubo erupted with a series of titanic explosions on June 15 and 16, blowing 500 feet off its 5,700-foot-high summit. The blasts plastered two cubic miles of rock over the surrounding countryside, and sent another cubic mile of ash (very fine rock dust) into the air—some of which blew 25 miles up and fell 1,500 miles away. Pinatubo's human toll was as excessive as its geological impact—over 700 lives gone, 108,000 homes destroyed, and more than a million people left without places to live or work. The misery was compounded by a typhoon that swept the area the very day the volcano erupted!

Terrible as it was, all this ash and rock and devastated landscape had little effect on the world's weather. Most of the ash settled out of the atmosphere within days of the eruption and never had a chance to foul the climate. What did stay up, though, were clouds of sulfur dioxide gas shot into the sky along with the ash. Sulfur dioxide is the same noxious gas that comes from coal-burning factories and power plants and gives us acid rain. Pinatubo blew several million tons of the stuff into the atmosphere, much of which continued on up into the stratosphere. The stratosphere is that part of the atmosphere lying between about eight and 30 miles up. It is a pretty quiet place, and once gases get there, they stay for months or years.

As a gas, sulfur dioxide is transparent, but in the stratosphere it combines with water vapor to form little droplets of sulfuric acid—the same corrosive material that forms the clouds shrouding the planet Venus. Fortunately, Earth's sulfuric acid clouds never get as dense as Venus's, although after Pinatubo they were thick enough to blot out 2 to 5 percent of the sun's rays. Similarly thick clouds formed after the eruptions of Krakatoa (Indonesia, 1883), Santa Maria (Guatemala, 1902), Katmai (Alaska, 1912), Agung (Indonesia, 1963), and El Chichon (Mexico, 1982). In 1815 Indonesia hosted the most recent major blow, when Tambora exploded with 50 times the force of Mount Saint Helens. The sulfur cloud from Tambora is estimated to have been five times as thick as Pinatubo's, and may have cut the solar energy reaching the ground by as much as 20 percent.

It's not hard to see these clouds of sulfuric acid if you look at the right time. At 15 miles up, they catch the last rays of sunlight long after the ground has slipped into darkness, resulting in brilliant lavender twilights about 20 minutes before sunrise and after sunset. Spectacular twilights were seen worldwide for several years after each of the big eruptions of the past century, including Pinatubo.

Theoretically, trimming the amount of sunlight by two or three percent should cool the surface of the earth. The amount of solar energy reaching the latitude of Michigan drops off by 3 percent every two days during the autumn, due to the lowering sun angle. Over these two days, Michigan's average temperature will normally cool about three-quarters of a degree. We might expect a similar cooling following a big eruption. The volcanic cooling should last as long as the volcanic cloud does—one or two years—and begin six to nine months after the eruption, as soon as the dust cloud has spread around the globe. Furthermore, according to some authorities, the cooling should be greatest in the Arctic and Antarctic, where the already feeble sunlight would suffer the greatest dimming from the dust; also, up in the Arctic the cooling would be most noticeable in the summer. (The sun doesn't shine there in the winter, so the dust wouldn't make any difference!)

Volcanic cooling gives Michigan colder cold fronts coming down from Canada and points north during the summer, leading to July frosts and a lack of heat waves—which is exactly what happened in 1992. So that Philippine volcano could very well be the culprit in Michigan's "year without a summer". But, wait, not so fast—the last big volcanic blowout, 1982's El Chichon, was followed by an exceptionally hot summer in '83, while the summer of 1964, one year after the eruption of Agung, was just about normal. Meanwhile, Michigan's coldest summers before 1992 (1915, 1950, and 1982) happened without any volcanic dust to blame. (El Chichon's dust hadn't spread far enough north by the summer of 1982 to have any effect.)

Going farther back in time, old records at Fort Brady (Sault Ste. Marie) reveal that the summer of 1837 was even colder (by 1 degree) than the summer of 1992, and it came on the heels of a bitterly cold winter and spring. It also followed the massive eruption of Coseguina (in Nicaragua) by a couple of years. Also, a six-year cold spell in the 1880s coincides with the infamous explosion of Krakatoa (west of Java), and several later eruptions around the world. And, last but not least, the greatest volcanic detonation in centuries, Tambora (east of Java) in 1815, was followed by the most famous "Year Without a Summer"—1816. There are no weather records from Michigan to describe the weather at the time, but in New England and Europe all fingers point to an exceptionally cold year. At Philadelphia it was the coldest it had been in the past 250 years! Of course, there *was* a summer in 1816, but not much of one— frequent frosts and the general lack of warm growing weather resulted in widespread crop failures north and east of the Potomac. Many farmers packed up and crossed the Alleghenies to the Ohio Valley (and no doubt a few continued on to Michigan), in hopes of finding more reliable growing conditions.

This lengthy and somewhat inconclusive account of volcanic eruptions and cold years (and summers) has a point: While not all volcanoes lead to cold summers and not all cold summers follow major volcanoes, it appears that the greatest eruptions of the past two centuries—Tambora, Coseguina, Krakatoa, and Pinatubo—may have led to cold summers a year or two later. Naturally, not all the details fit perfectly (such as cool summers occurring right *before* an eruption!), but there is enough coincidence to feed the suspicion that a geologic upheaval half a world away led to July frosts in Sault Ste. Marie!

IS MICHIGAN GETTING WARMER...?

Perhaps it seems strange to talk about volcanoes and climate cooling when there's so much discussion of "global warming" in the news and among politicians. Has the "greenhouse effect," the feared warming of our planet due to gases released into the atmosphere by factories and fires, finally arrived? Along the same line, were winters *really* snowier when your grandmother was a kid? These are interesting and important issues, but before we jump into the question of climate change, it makes sense to describe what climate *is*.

Climate is not the same as weather. Weather is the state of the atmosphere—temperature, pressure, wind, cloudiness, where it's raining and where it isn't, the positions of highs, lows, and fronts on the weather map, and many other factors—at any given moment. Weather, of course, is *always* changing! Climate, on the other hand, is the overall average of weather over a long period of time. A complete description of the climate is not just a bunch of averages, but also includes a description of the variability of the weather from day to day, from summer to winter, and from year to year. After all, Detroit's temperature can stray rather far from its annual average of 49°, and nobody is surprised when one year averages several degrees warmer or colder than the previous year.

It's trite but true that nothing is so constant as change, and climatologists recognize this. However, any definition that considers the Great Ice Age, the steamy era of the dinosaurs, and the present as all being part of the same climate isn't very practical (you wouldn't know whether to grow apples, bananas, or frozen peas). While one exceptionally rainy spring or bitter winter, or even a "year without a summer," does not mean a change of climate, the melting of Michigan's mile-deep ice 10,000 years ago obviously does. There must be a happy medium somewhere; the World Meteorological Organization, along with the National Weather Service and National Oceanographic and Atmospheric Administration, have concurred that averages taken over a 30-year period give the most useful definition of climate. The local climate data table in this book are averages for 1951 through 1980; in 1993, averages for 1961 through 1990 can be considered the norm for world climate. There's nothing magic about 30 years—many climatologists think 10 years works just as well. In either case, the averaging period is long enough to smooth out the large year-to-year fluctuations and reduce the impact of one-time extremes, but not so long as to mask important long-term changes of, say, rainfall patterns. Furthermore, a 10-to 30-year average gives us a better guess of next year's weather than a 5-year or 50-year average does.

Enough generalities—let's get specific. The British took temperatures at Fort Detroit from 1781 to 1786, but except for some intermittent observations around 1820, the Americans didn't resume the readings until 1839. Over the years, Detroit grew from a fort to a metropolitan area of 5 million people, and in 1958 the "official" thermometer was moved from downtown to the airport—changes that make it impossible to detect any real climate trends in Detroit's record.

Fortunately for Michigan's climate watchers, the Surgeon General of the U.S. Army, Dr. James Tilton, decided back in 1814 that it would be a good idea for weather records to be taken at their remote outposts in the Northwest Territories. One of the most isolated stations was established at the outlet of Lake Superior in January 1823. The site of Fort Brady is only a few miles from what is now Sault Ste. Marie. Running a weather station (or a fort) in Sault Ste. Marie in 1823 wasn't an easy job. But despite disease, lousy food, bugs in the summer and cold quarters in the winter, the post's Assistant Surgeon faithfully recorded temperature and weather conditions three times a day. This rugged beginning marks the start of the longest and most useful climate record in the Michigan Territory.

The record at Sault Ste. Marie isn't perfect either—there's a big gap from 1857 to 1888, which I filled in using temperature observations from Marquette and Alpena (appropriately adjusted, of course). But Sault Ste. Marie is still a small town, without the urban "heat island" effect that raises the temperature of Detroit several degrees above that of the surrounding countryside. Sault Ste. Marie, then, is a good place to look for global warming—or at least Michigan warming—and to see if the "greenhouse effect" has arrived.

SAULT STE. MARIE AVERAGE ANNUAL TEMPERATURES

Yearly and 30-Year Averages, 1823-1992

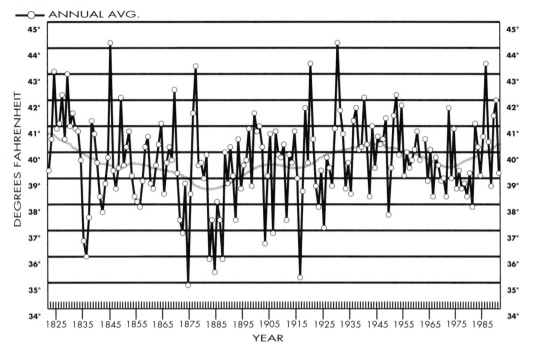

To many in upper Michigan, especially after the summer of '92, the greenhouse effect may not seem like such a bad idea. The basic premise is that the sun heats the earth, which radiates its excess heat back into space. The balance between incoming sunlight and outgoing radiation determines the average temperature of the planet. Certain gases in the atmosphere, notably carbon dioxide, absorb the outgoing radiation and block the escape of heat to space—in much the same manner as the glass roof of a greenhouse. And as in a greenhouse, the earth warms beneath the blanket of carbon dioxide. The theory was first proposed in 1863, and meteorologists have been looking for its effects ever since.

We know the greenhouse effect works—just look at the planet Venus. Venus's atmosphere has 260,000 times more carbon dioxide than does Earth's—a typical thermometer reading there would be 855° Fahrenheit. That reading is far higher than it would be if Venus had Earth's atmosphere. Back on Earth, the amount of carbon dioxide in our atmosphere is increasing, thanks (in part) to the burning of oil and forests. So far, the increase has been relatively modest—about 20 percent in the past century. Theoretically, the warming over the past century due to carbon dioxide should have been about a degree, plus or minus, with larger rises projected over the next few decades as more carbon dioxide is dumped into the air.

Well, that's the theory. But nature doesn't always behave to our expectations, so it's worthwhile to look at the climate to see what the atmosphere itself thinks of global warming. It sounds so simple—just gather all these old temperature readings from Fort Brady and Sault Ste. Marie, average them to get an annual mean temperature, plot them on a graph, and see if it's getting warmer or colder. There are complications, however. While the exact details are lost to history, the Fort Brady thermometer was probably mounted on the north wall of the dispensary building; nowadays thermometers are placed in ventilated boxes to shield them from direct sunlight. Furthermore, for the first 32 years the Fort Brady readings were taken three times a day, at 7 A.M., 2 P.M., and 9 P.M., the idea being to catch the morning low temperature, the afternoon maximum, and an in-between temperature in the evening. The average of the three readings was taken to be the daily mean temperature. In the late 1800s thermometers registering the highest and lowest temperatures of the day became widely available; since then, meteorologists have been averaging these high and low readings for the daily mean. The results of the two methods are not always the same, even at the same location on the same day! Fortunately, once these differences in weather observing techniques are known, they can be taken into consideration to derive an "adjusted," and we hope, improved temperature record (which, again, I've done). While all this may sound like mere minutia, I've mentioned it to show that annual temperatures, be they for Fort Brady or averages for the world, are not necessarily precise. This should give you something to think about before believing that a 1° climate change is "real." Don't forget that numbers like these are being used to predict planetary catastrophes and influence national and global energy policies!

Now, finally, let's look at the numbers. Perhaps the most striking thing about the annual temperatures is how much they can change from one year to the next. The warmest years, 1846 and 1931, ran 10 degrees warmer than 1875, the coldest year—a climate change equivalent to moving from Monroe (Michigan's warmest place) to Champion (the state's coldest location). The warmest years, 1931, 1846, 1921, 1987, and 1878, are pretty well scattered throughout the 170-year record, while the coldest years, 1875, 1917, 1885, 1888, and 1883, point out a cold spell in the late 1800s. Remarkable temperature swings occurred during 1843-47 and 1875-79, when annual temperatures steadily rose by 9 degrees over three years, then plummeted back to normal levels after the fourth year. Simply stated, be wary of thinking that several warm or cold years means a real trend.

Speaking of trends, the graph's smooth, heavy line shows a running 30-year average of annual temperatures—essentially, a year-by-year account of the changing climate. Amazingly, over the 170 years from 1823 to 1992 there is essentially no net change in Sault Ste. Marie's "normal" temperature, with the first 30 years averaging a mere one-tenth of a degree colder than the last 30 years! That doesn't mean the Soo's climate has been steady throughout For the first 60 years temperatures dropped by 2 degrees, bottoming out around 1880. Then things warmed back up for the next 60 years, peaking around 1940, prompting the first scientific claims (in 1939) that greenhouse warming was to blame. Temperatures underwent a 1-degree dip in the 1960s and 1970s, and by 1992 the "normal" temperature was back up where it was in 1823 and 1940. For mathematical reasons, each 30-year average is accurate only to about half a degree, so it's quite possible that the one-half and one-degree wiggles in the temperature curve since 1900 are meaningless statistical flukes.

A century of statewide temperatures, compiled by the National Climatic Data Center in Asheville, North Carolina, averaged from dozens of weather stations all across Michigan, shows pretty much the same thing—perhaps some slight cooling since 1888, but so slight that it doesn't mean anything. At Eastern Michigan University in Ypsilanti, Professors Carl Ojala and Robert Ferrett examined climate trends over the past century at 45 individual locations, and found more mixed results—38 locations warmed between 1898 and 1955, and 33 of them cooled from 1955 to 1990. The other dozen or so places either had no significant changes, or cooled when the rest of the state warmed and vice versa! The E.M.U. researchers also noted that all but six of the 45 weather stations moved (across town, out to the airport, etc.) during the years studied, further complicating the results. The bottom line is that if there is such a thing as global warming, it hasn't showed up in Michigan yet.

Climate is not just simple averages. Actually, extremes are more interesting than averages, and what could be more extreme than the highest and lowest temperatures recorded anywhere in the state each year? If you're wondering whether summers are growing hotter or if winters are getting colder, a peek at some extreme temperatures might give you a clue. Just keep in mind the usual word of caution—that a single heat wave or cold snap doesn't always mean an exceptional summer or winter. Prior to 1888 there weren't enough weather stations in Michigan to provide meaningful statewide extremes; the yearly highs and lows since then show no distinct trends to hotter hots or colder colds, nor is there any clear-cut moderation in the extremes. There was, however, an outstanding stretch of extreme weather from 1911 through 1936, when ten years saw temperatures reach 105° or higher somewhere in the state and 8 years had readings of -45° or lower. Outside of that quarter century, years with extremes as high as 105° or as low as -45° are almost as scarce as hen's teeth—only three of each.

The climate showed its tendency for extremes in the mid-1930s. Michigan's all-time high of 112° arrived in 1936, a year that was, on average, 2 degrees colder than average. Meanwhile, just two years earlier, -51° was the coldest ever. The 159-degree *range* of temperatures in 1934, from -51° to 108°, was the greatest in Michigan's history. The decade of the 1930s was also the Michigan's driest. But why all this happened, and if or when it will happen again—well, nobody has a clue.

...OR WETTER?

To many, especially farmers, rainfall is a more important element of the climate than temperature. While cold waves, blizzards, tornadoes, floods, and other dramatic events leave the most vivid impressions on those in their paths, it is really the protracted spells of rather uninteresting weather known as drought that have the greatest effect on humanity. In terms of total human suffering and economic loss, the greatest natural disaster ever to befall the United States was not a hurricane, a tornado, the eruption of Mount Saint Helens, or even the San Francisco Earthquake, but the 1930s "Dust Bowl," a severe, seven-year drought that turned the Great Plains states from Texas to the Dakotas into near-deserts. Fortunately, Michigan was on the edge of the Dust Bowl, and its drought was comparatively minor.

Rainfall records are lot trickier to translate than are temperature records. A single downpour at Fort Brady, or anywhere else, could push annual precipitation way above normal, while drought reigns generally throughout the state. For example: at the height of the "Dust Bowl" years, 1934 was one of Michigan's driest years on record, but a few weeks of heavy but localized lake-effect snows in November gave Sault Ste. Marie an above-average total precipitation for the year. So we'll look at the 105 years of statewide precipitation (which includes melted snowfall along with rain) averaged over many rainfall reporting stations all across Michigan.

As with temperature, precipitation shows its greatest variability from year to year, with long-term trends changing more sedately. The wettest year, 1985, had nearly twice as much precipitation as 1930, the driest year. There are cases of extremely dry years being followed by very wet years, as in 1930 and 1931, 1958 and 1959, and 1989 and 1990, and wet years followed by dry ones (such as 1929 and 1930, and 1975 and 1976). Multi-year dry spells of 1934-36, 1962-65, and 1987-89 resulted in the worst droughts of the century, with crop failures, low wells, and urban water shortages.

On the longer view, Michigan is a distinctly wetter place now than it was a century ago. Statewide average precipitation has increased about 10 percent since the late 1800s, with the increase interrupted by the droughts of the 1930s and 1960s. Longer records from Detroit, Fort Brady, and a few other locations indicate that Michigan's climate was somewhat wetter before 1890 than it is now. However, rain gauges were few and far between back then, so for confirmation we'll turn to the "World's Largest Rain Gauge,"—the Great Lakes.

The water level of each Great Lake depends on many factors, such as water inflow from streams and other lakes, outflow at the other end of the lake, evaporation, man-made diversions (at Chicago and Buffalo), and consumption by humans, animals, crops, lawns, and industry. The most important factor by far, however, is precipitation—rain and snow that falls directly on the lake, as well as that which falls in the watershed area that drains into the lake.

Except for a few square miles along the Wisconsin border in Gogebic and Iron Counties, all of Michigan's waters flow into the Great Lakes. The large majority of that water ends up in Lakes Michigan and Huron, which, being connected through the Straits of Mackinac, are really one big happy lake. The lakes rise during rainy years and fall when the weather dries out. Because of the lakes' enormous size, it take three to four years of abnormal precipitation to make a real impact on the water levels. In general, if Michigan's statewide precipitation over the past three or four years has averaged one inch more than normal, Lakes Michigan and Huron will run about a foot deeper than normal. The lakes fell two or three feet during the droughts of the 1930s and 1960s, and rose to near-record levels after the wet years of the mid-1980s. These fluctuations in Michigan's water budget were the largest of the past century, but if you spend a few moments comparing the records of lake levels and statewide precipitation, you'll see that most of the lesser dips and peaks also correspond remarkably well.

It's too bad there wasn't much of a rain-gauge network in Michigan before 1888, because the lakes tell us that the climate was much wetter then. For the period 1860 through 1890, Lakes Michigan and Huron stood one to three feet above the 20th century's average level—about the same as the recent record levels of the mid-1980s. This suggests that Michigan's wettest year on record—1985—would have been nothing unusual in the mid-1800s. The high lake levels also lend credence to some 19th century precipitation measurements that seem preposterous by today's standards, such as the 71.19 inches recorded at Detroit in 1855 and two-year totals exceeding 110 inches at Cooper Center (near Kalamazoo) in 1861-62 and at Adrian in 1881-82.

Going back even earlier, we find that Michigan's climate was wetter yet! The highest recorded level of Lakes Michigan and Huron was measured in 1838, nearly five feet above present averages. Geological evidence, such as ancient beaches left high and dry, flooded tree stumps and stream beds, etc., says that even 1838's high water mark was down from the levels that prevailed for centuries, from 1000 A.D. until around 1800. Except for a break around 1250 to 1500 A.D., lake levels ran five to ten feet above today's norms, giving Michigan at that time a climate similar to that of present-day New York. For three centuries before that, from 700 to 1000 A.D., the lakes stood about five feet *lower* than they do now—implying that Michigan averaged only about 26 inches of precipitation per year, about the same as Minnesota today.

Looking farther back in geologic history is risky, since the drainage patterns in and out of the lakes may have been quite different, and changes in lake levels probably had other causes than climate. These ancient lake levels, however, tell us that the climate fluctuations we've witnessed over the past century are minor compared to what can happen should the climate really decide to change!

Note: The record of lake levels before 1761 comes from "A stratigraphic study of beach features on the southwestern shore of Lake Michigan: New evidence of Holocene lake level fluctuations," by Curtis E. Larsen (1985), Environmental Geology Notes 112, Illinois State Geological Survey, Natural Resource Building, 615 East Peabody Drive, Champaign, IL 61820.

WHAT ABOUT SNOW?

Now, to the ultimate question about climate change, a question that has torn families apart. Were winters *really* snowier when your grandmother (or mother) was a kid? Well, it all depends on which peninsula you call home. In the middle of the Lower Peninsula, East Lansing's seasonal snowfall has slowly declined since records began in 1864. The first 64 winters at East Lansing averaged 48" of snow, while the average for the last 64 winters dropped to 43". The story is just the opposite up at Sault Ste. Marie, where snowfall records began in 1888. There the average snowfall has *increased* steadily over the past century, from 78" for the first 52 winters to 137" since 1940. Remarkably, with only two exceptions, each of the past ten decades at Sault Ste. Marie was snowier than the previous decade!

Of course, as with all climate data, snowfall records should be taken with a grain of rock salt. Measuring techniques, such as whether newly fallen snow is measured every hour or just once a day, along with observer diligence, local terrain and buildings (which affect drifting), and, of course, that great bane of climate data—whether the snow is measured in town or at

LANSING'S BIG SNOW
January 27, 1967

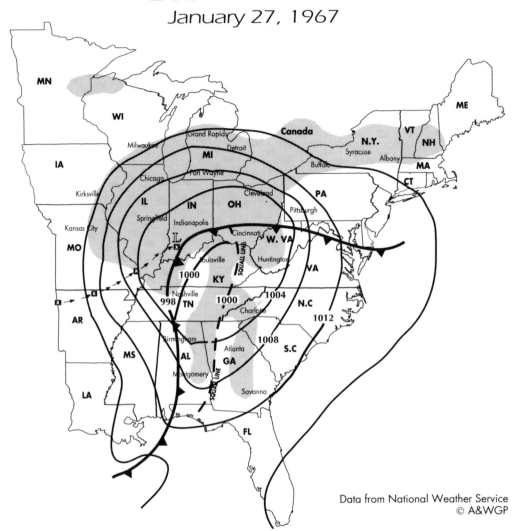

Data from National Weather Service
© A&WGP

the airport—can all influence snowfall totals. Michigan's snowfall record, however, shows consistent enough patterns over the past century to suggest that real changes are going on. In general, the greatest increases in snowfall have been in the snowbelt areas east of Lake Michigan and (especially) south of Lake Superior; the most marked decreases have been in southeastern Michigan (including Detroit and Lansing). Perhaps nature is being kind for a change, by dumping less snow on the streets of Metro Detroit and more on the ski runs of the Upper Peninsula!

THE GREAT ICE AGE

You might have noticed that I keep coming back to a basic problem with climate data: the inaccuracies and inconsistencies in weather measurements over the years, and how resulting errors in climate statistics may be as large as real climate changes. It's a real quandary for climatologists, since there's intense interest from many sides—government agencies, the media, industry, agriculture, the public, and grandmothers—in definite "yes" or "no" answers to questions like the greenhouse effect and whether or not winters are snowier than in years past. The odds are that simple yes or no answers won't be available until we have accumulated many more years of accurate climate observations, or until the greenhouse (or some other) effect becomes unmistakably large.

But enough of these mere hiccups in the earth's climate. Let's talk about the granddaddy of them all—the Great Ice Age. No worries about inaccurate thermometers and half-degree temperature differences here—the evidence is literally carved in stone all across Michigan. On a steamy August afternoon it might seem inconceivable that only 18,000 years earlier (a mere blink of an eye, geologically speaking), all of Michigan was buried under one or two miles of solid ice (in January it might seem a little more believable). Other ice sheets covered northern Europe, from Britain to Russia, and Antarctica.

The greatest ice sheet of all time formed around Hudson's Bay and spread across half of North America. Glacier ice extended as far south as St. Louis, Missouri, with the Ohio and Missouri rivers marking its southernmost boundaries. Michigan literally owes its existence to the Ice Age—the basins that are now the Great Lakes were scoured out by the ground-plowing glaciers, and the rocky debris was deposited in huge gravel banks all across Michigan.

Apparently there were many ice ages—various counts range from four or five to twenty or more. The whole mess started about 2 million years ago, and the ice has advanced and retreated every 100,000 years or so ever since. It's hard to tell how many of the glacial advances reached Michigan, since each one effectively erased the geological evidence of the previous glaciers. Between each of these ice ages the climate was much like it is today. The last round began 80 or 90 thousand years ago, and the ice sheet reached its maximum size 18,000 years ago (or 16,000 B.C.). Around 12,000 B.C. the world's climate suddenly warmed up to near present temperatures, and the Big Melt began. Michigan's last glacial ice disappeared around 10,000 B.C. It took another 5,000 years to melt the rest of the huge mass of ice, and the last patch disappeared from northern Quebec around 5,000 B.C. The Ice Age still lives in Antarctica and Greenland, and remnant icecaps dot some islands of northeastern Canada.

Today's Michigan landscape is littered with geological relics from the Ice Age. Exposed rocks along the shores of Lake Superior show the smooth, striated polishing action of the moving ice, while chunks of copper-bearing rock from the Keweenaw Peninsula rode the glaciers to Iowa. Moraines, those piles of leftover gravel, are scattered across much of lower Michigan (Lake Michigan's dunes are made of moraine gravel). Chunks of ice left in the gravel by the retreating glaciers melted into water-filled depressions called "kettle ponds," while rocks left by melt water in glacial crevasses became long, gravely ridges known as "eskers" (such as Blue Ridge, on Highway 127 about 6 miles south of Jackson). And the valley of the Grand River in central Michigan used to be Lake Huron's exit to the sea (via Lake Michigan and the Chicago, Illinois, and Mississippi Rivers). Actually, you'd be hard pressed to find terrain in Michigan that was NOT shaped by glaciers!

Needless to say, the Michigan's ice-age climate was quite different from today's. Exactly how different is a matter of some speculation, but combining geologic clues with some logical deductions based on modern meteorology, we can guess what it was like. Obviously, it was cold—especially when the entire state was buried in ice. Also, since the temperature difference between the Arctic and the tropics was larger—that's what drives the wind—it was probably quite windy. Geologic evidence for wind includes deep deposits of dust, known as "loess," blown into the Mississippi and Ohio valleys from the arid plains to the west. With so much water locked up in the ice sheets, the world's oceans were 300 feet shallower than they are today, and Michigan's prime source of moisture—the Gulf of Mexico—was much smaller and cooler. Thus, Michigan was probably a lot drier during the Ice Age.

That's what happened; now the question is: Why? There are many theories explaining the ice ages, and some of them may actually be true. One plausible idea put forth in 1920 by a Serb named Milankovitch concerns the wobbles of the earth and its orbit. Like a spinning top, the axis of Earth's poles wobbles around and changes its tilt in cycles of 26,000 and 40,000 years, while the shape of the earth's orbit around the sun changes over several longer cycles—up to 100,000 years. The actual size of the orbit never changes, and, over an entire year, the total amount of sunlight reaching the earth never changes. However, the wobbles vary the amount of sunlight reaching the different hemispheres during different seasons by 5 or 10 percent over thousands of years. When the northern hemisphere gets less summer sunlight, that season is cooler. As it is now, the winter snows that cover the far north barely melt before summer is over; if summers were 5° cooler, the snow might not melt at all. New snow would fall on the old, and the snow layer would build up year after year. When the snow gets deep enough it increases the cooling by reflecting sunlight back into space. Keep that up for a few thousand years and you've got an ice age.

The Milankovitch theory predicts several possible ice-age cycles, some of them close to the observed 100,000-year (plus or minus) cycle. The theory also predicts that the past ice age was not the last one, and that the next one could start in 5,000 or 10,000 years.

There's another, and somewhat unnerving, idea that ice ages can start suddenly and without warning. It has to do with the "natural variability" mentioned at the start of this chapter, and how "abnormally" cold summers or snowy winters are merely part of the normal variability of climate. If, by chance, the world has a sequence of several *extremely* cold summers and snowy winters (at the limits of but still within the range of "normal"), arctic ice sheets can start to grow without having to wait for the earth to wobble. It need not take long—a few years, perhaps—to build up a layer of snow that's big enough to reflect a lot of sunlight and deep enough to survive the summer, and once that happens, the next ice age could be on. The chances of this happening in any given year (say, next year) are very, very small, but then, ice ages don't happen every year either. And there's always the possibility that a round of huge volcanic eruptions could provide enough cool summers to trigger the big freeze...

All this raises the possibility of a titanic duel between the Milankovitch and greenhouse effects, with "natural variability" and a few volcanoes thrown in as wild cards. At stake is a climate that ends in either fire or ice. Stay tuned!

THE AURORA: NIGHT LIGHTS OF THE NORTH COUNTRY

There are many ways to spend a clear night; one of the finest is to watch the aurora borealis, or northern lights. This is particularly true in Michigan, where auroras are fairly frequent, and especially during the winter, when the otherwise long and dark nights might seem to have little else to offer. However, the northern lights are a audiovisual delight any time of year—watch one reflecting off the still waters of a lake while loons provide background music and you'll know what I mean!

Displays of the aurora often begin as a pale green arch hugging the northern horizon, and many nights the show never progresses beyond this stage. Some nights, though, searchlight beams grow out of the glow and crisscross the sky, multiplying and merging into red and green curtains that march overhead and off to the south. At times, the entire sky may shine and shimmer like an incongruous mixture of fire and jello. Kind of gives you goose bumps just thinking about it, doesn't it?

Of course, we know the aurora is neither fire nor jello, but for centuries the actual cause of these lights was a complete mystery. The word "aurora" means "dawn" in Latin and "borealis" means "north"; Down Under, the southern equivalent is the "aurora australis." Since the days of Aristotle in ancient Greece, the most acceptable explanations of the "northern dawn" involved peculiar kinds of twilight—for example, sunlight reflecting off polar ice back into the sky. Auroras were also blamed on distant forest fires illuminating the sky, or even spontaneous combustion of the air itself. It wasn't until the beginning of this century, when the first rudiments of atomic physics were being worked out, that the true cause of the aurora came to light.

Auroras work on the same basic principle as fluorescent or neon lights, or outdoor mercury and sodium vapor lamps. The gas—neon, mercury, or sodium—glows when energetic, high speed electrons are run through it. In the case of the aurora, the gases are mostly oxygen and nitrogen (the main constituents of air). High speed electrons strike the gas molecules, jolting the molecules' electrons out of their tiny orbits. When the molecular electrons drop back to their original orbits, they lose the energy they picked up from the high-speed electrons. This energy radiates away as light.

The high speed electrons in fluorescent lights come from the house current, with an extra kick given by the lamp's ballast mechanism. The aurora is lit by electrons from the sun, which need no boost. Electrons thrown out by hot spots in the solar atmosphere known as solar flares can travel the 93 million miles to earth in less than a day, zipping along at 1,000 miles per second for most of their journey. But, several thousand miles short of their target—Earth—they get caught in our planet's magnetic field. This magnetic field has broad loops connecting the north and south poles, just like the familiar pattern around a bar magnet. The electrons are deflected north or south along these loops, dipping down into the atmosphere as they approach the poles. To an electron, the magnetic field looks somewhat like an apple, with electrons on the surface of the apple moving "north" or "south" into one of the dimples. The electrons are finally funneled into the top of the atmosphere in a ring (called the "auroral oval") surrounding each of the magnetic poles.

Electrons are always funneling down to earth, and there's always an aurora—albeit faint most of the time—along the auroral oval. But some of the extremely energetic electrons shot from solar flares penetrate much deeper into the magnetic field before getting caught. Their trajectories bring them into the atmosphere farther from the poles, the (northern) auroral oval expands south, and we see the northern lights.

The same electrons that create such beauty in the sky can wreak havoc on earth. Disturbances in the earth's magnetic field brought on by all this electricity can induce electrical currents in long metal objects such as telephone wires, power lines, and pipelines, leading to power outages and communications disruptions. A "magnetic storm" in 1989 knocked out the power grid for the entire province of Quebec. Long-distance radio communications may be wiped out as electrons alter the upper atmosphere's ability to reflect radio waves at certain frequencies (particularly short-wave). It has even been suggested that solar disturbances may trigger storm development and influence droughts, but these theories are quite controversial among meteorologists.

The aurora gives us a chance to glimpse the very highest reaches of our atmosphere. Most auroras shine between 60 and 200 miles up, but occasionally a really big show can reach as high as 600 miles—higher than most satellites! In contrast to these enormous vertical dimensions, the curtains themselves are only a few thousand feet thick. Often the curtains shade from greenish on the bottom to red at the top; both colors come from oxygen atoms. Occasionally a deep violet glow from nitrogen atoms appears in the higher reaches of the aurora.

The north and south poles of earth's magnet—the dimples on the apple, so to speak—are not exactly at the geographic north and south poles, but about 1,000 miles away. That places the magnetic north pole over Ellesmere Island in the Canadian Arctic. This quirk of our magnetic field is a boon for Michigan aurora watchers, since it brings the magnetic north pole—and the auroral oval—1,000 miles closer, increasing the frequency of auroras. In Mongolia, which is at the same geographic latitude as Michigan but 2,000 miles farther from the magnetic north pole, auroras are much less frequent than they are in Michigan.

Over North America the auroral oval usually runs from northern Alaska, across the northern Northwest Territories, into northern Quebec and Labrador. That's the place to go if you want to see the aurora almost every clear night. Farther south, the frequency drops off—to 30 nights a year in northern Michigan, and about half that for southern Michigan. Ambitious aurora watchers far from city lights may be able to see even more than these statistics indicate. The southernmost aurora borealis on record was seen from the Cayman Islands (19 degrees north) in the Caribbean in March, 1989.

The very name "northern lights" associates auroras with cold places and long nights, and it might seem that they should be most frequent in winter. But solar flares care little about seasons on earth, and auroras can occur at any time of year. There is actually a noticeable preference for auroras to be seen during the equinoctial months of March, April, September, and October. Much more important than any seasonal variability is the effect of the "sunspot cycle," an 11-year cycle of solar activity (including solar flares). While some not very spectacular auroras may be seen throughout the sunspot cycle, the really big shows generally reserve themselves for the years right around the peak of the cycle. The last peak was about 1989 to 1991, when quite a few spectacular shows lit up the skies; the next peak should arrive around 2000.

MICHIGAN WEATHER EVENTS, 9,000 B.C. TO 1992 A.D.

■■■■■■■■■■■■■■■■■■■■■■■■■■■■

Michigan has a long and interesting—and occasionally violent—weather history. Here's a selection of the more outstanding events, some of which you may have lived through, and many more you may have heard about. There may be a few events that you thought never happened in Michigan. So, if this year's weather seems freakish, don't worry—a glance through this list will show that Michigan's weather is *always* freakish!

9000 B.C. The Great Lakes (and Michigan) form as ice-age glaciers retreat to the north. (See reference on page 101.)

3000 B.C. Lakes Michigan and Huron reach their highest levels since the ice age, about 20' above present levels (deduced from elevations of ancient beaches). Whether the high waters were due to a wetter climate back then or to changes in the lakes' drainage patterns is unclear, but the levels fell when a new channel was carved at the south end of Lake Huron (this channel is now the St. Clair River).

700 to 1000 A.D. Lake Michigan and Huron levels fall to—and remain—about 5' below present levels, implying 3 centuries of drier and possibly warmer weather than we see now.

1000 to 1800 A.D. Lake levels run 5' to 10' above present levels, suggesting a cooler and wetter climate than today's. There was a break around 1250 to 1500 A.D. when Michigan's climate was similar to our present climate (maybe) and the lakes stood near present levels.

1781 In August, Dr. George C. Anthon, British Army Post Surgeon at Fort Detroit, Upper Canada, begins taking the first known records of Michigan's weather. He continued his daily "meteorological journal" for five years.

1784 Dr. Anthon records one of Detroit's most severe winters in history. Seven below zero on January 7 freezes the Detroit River, and temperatures fall to -15° or lower on January 9, 16, 25, and 27-30. The new month brings a thaw, but by February 8 and 9 it is back down to -12°. February ends with -10° on the 29th (probably Detroit's coldest leap-year day ever!). Readings of -6° and -4° on March 4 and 5 bring the winter's number of sub-zero mornings to 23!

1821 The Detroit *Gazette* reports temperatures of -27° upstate in March, and 8" of wet snow falling at Detroit on April 18.

1823 The U.S. Army Post Surgeon at Fort Brady, just west of Sault Ste. Marie in the

Michigan Territory, starts keeping his "Diary of the Weather." In February his thermometer dips to -30°. The average for the month is but 8.9°, and the warmest all month is a meager 33°. The Fort Brady record continued for 32 years.

1826 Thirty-seven below in February at Fort Brady matches the 20th century low for Sault Ste. Marie set in 1934.

1827 Fort Brady musters only a high of 84° for the summer.

1834 The winter's low at Fort Brady is a mild -12°. Michigan's first recorded tornado is reported near Detroit in February. Another tornado at Kalamazoo on October 18 destroys some buildings but causes no injuries. Around noon one summer day, the St. Marys River at Sault Ste. Marie suddenly empties and, an hour later, just as suddenly fills back up. Many who go out to catch stranded fish narrowly escape the returning surge, apparently a seiche.

1836 A protracted winter, which starts early in November 1835 and lingers into April 1837, creates all sorts of problems for settlers whose food and supplies run out before the arrival of spring in May. Every month from November through May is colder than normal at Fort Brady, and in histories of the time the winter becomes known as "the starving time." According to the Indian ethnologist at the Soo, Henry Rowe Schoolcraft, "February 1 the mercury fell to 40 below zero. This is the extreme on the graduated scale I have—it fell nearly into the ball."

1837 The winter and spring of 1836-37 are even colder than those of the previous year. Fort Brady's thermometer bottoms out at -30° in February. Summer (June-August) averages only 56.8°, which is 5° below normal and the coldest ever.

1838 A wet summer in the Great Lakes region lifts the waters of Lakes Michigan and Huron to 584' above sea level in July, 4.5' above the 20th century average and 1.7' higher than peak levels in 1986. The high waters were the last hurrah of the long wet spell that began around 1000 A.D.

1839 The mercury soars to 96 in July at Fort Brady.

1843 March averages of 12.1° at Fort Brady and 22.5° at Detroit are 5° colder than an average January, on the heels of a February that was 7° below normal. At Edwardsburg in southwest Michigan, snow lies 2' deep at the end of March, and sledding continues until April 8 in the Detroit area. On April 3 ducks are spotted heading back south over Detroit, having foolishly flown north the week before. Thousands of cattle starve as hay supplies run out. Springlike weather finally arrives around April 10, but Lake Erie doesn't open for navigation until May 6. A warm summer brings a good crop season.

1845 Detroit's winter (December-February) of 1844-45 is the second mildest of the 19th century, averaging 32.8°. A 20-foot-high seiche on Lake Superior is reported at Copper Harbor.

1846 An annual average temperature of 43.6° at Fort Brady makes this the second-warmest year in history at Sault Ste. Marie. Every month of the year was warmer than normal.

1848 The *United States* and other steamers cruise Lake Erie between Buffalo, Cleveland, and Detroit in February as mild winter weather prevails.

1851 Fort Mackinac records only 11.70" of precipitation all year, but the reading is suspect—only 47 miles away, Fort Brady has 45.30".

1853 Temperatures reportedly soar to 106° at Detroit on June 22 and at Fort Brady on June 23, unofficial extreme records for both locations.

1855 Up to 3' of snow buries the snowbelt at the south end of Lake Michigan on January 21. Tornadoes strike Lapeer County on May 16 and Charlotte on May 23. Detroit is soaked by 71.19" of precipitation, the most ever measured in one year in Michigan. June and July bring 26.67", and 9.21" falls in November.

1857 Detroit remains continuously below freezing from December 29 (1856) until January 31, when the mercury rises to 37°. At 13.9°, it is Detroit's coldest January until 1912 comes along. Detroit's lowest is -12°, while Battle Creek is -26° on the 18th.

1860 A huge waterspout, last of a series of tornadoes that began in Iowa, is sighted from ships on southern Lake Michigan on the evening of June 4. Damaging winds from the same storm system strike near Grand Haven later that night.

1861 Marquette drops to -33° on February 7.

1863 A "violent hurricane" (possibly a tornado) rips sails and snaps masts on ships in Thunder Bay, near Alpena, on August 21.

1864 The New Year brings more rough weather to Alpena, as a powerful storm sends the barometer there down to 28.40" at 1 A.M. on January 1. At Detroit, the temperature falls from 40° to below zero as the storm's cold front passes overnight, and Marquette reports a daytime temperature of -18° that falls to -31° that night (-35° at the mines). The rest of winter is rather mild, though, and a sunny 60° is reported from Springwells (near Detroit) on January 27.

1866 Tornadoes touch down near Owosso and St. Johns on June 25.

1868 On February 2, the mercury dips to -37° at Lansing, the lowest ever recorded there. Monroe records -21° the next day.

1869 A brisk autumn in Lansing brings record lows of 30° in August and 7° in October.

1870 A "hurricane and hail storm of terrible fury" strikes Jonesville on June 20.

1871 A summer that brings only half the normal rainfall to much of Michigan (4.58" at Detroit, July-September) transforms vast expanses of debris left over from logging operations into a tinderbox. On October 9, fires set to clear the debris go on a rampage when whipped out of control by high winds ahead of a cold front, and by the next day 2.5 million acres of forest and an estimated 200 people are consumed by the flames across Michigan. More extreme in the list of casualties during the outbreak are Chicago, where another 200 die, and the town of Peshtigo in northeast Wisconsin, where 1,300 perish.

1872 An unofficial -33° at Grand Rapids on December 24, the coldest ever reported there.

1873 Heavy snow across southeast Michigan on January 22-23 is followed by a week of intense cold. Adrian reaches -30° on the 29th.

1875 January and February are the coldest consecutive two months in Michigan history, averaging 13.7° at Detroit and 4.6° at Marquette. The cold spell culminates with readings of -33° at Lansing and -37° at Traverse City on February 9, and an unbelievable -55° at Fort Brady (near Sault Ste. Marie) on February 13 and 14. Unfortunately, the Fort Brady readings lack sufficient documentation to be accepted as Michigan's all-time cold record. The cold pattern persisted all year, and every month averaged colder than normal at Detroit. When it was over,

1875 went down in the books as the coldest year on record at Detroit, Lansing, Escanaba, Marquette, and every other weather station in the state that kept records that year. Most places were about 1° colder than the next chilliest year, 1917.

A tornado struck northwest Detroit on June 27, wrecking houses in a 500-foot-wide path from 21st to 12th streets. Two people were killed.

1878 Arctic air avoids the upper Midwest this winter—Marquette's December-February average of 29.9° is a whopping 15° above normal, making the winter of 1877-78 the warmest ever! The warm winter may have been due to El Niño, a massive warmup of the Pacific Ocean that sends storms across the southern U.S. and into Alaska, but leaves the middle of the continent high and dry.

1880 Detroit records its earliest 0° reading on November 22.

1881 It is a wet year overall, especially in lower Michigan, where many places record 10" to 20" of surplus precipitation. The wettest place is Adrian, where 26" of precipitation in October, November, and December makes the year's total 64.01". The soggy autumn, however, comes too late to prevent one of Michigan's greatest disasters ever, a week of forest fires in the Thumb from August 31 to September 6. A dry August (1.32" at Detroit) combines with 100° heat to desiccate pine slashings left from logging operations and millions of fallen trunks from the 1871 fires. As in 1871, the inferno is ignited by land-clearing fires. When it is over, one million acres are burned, 20 villages gone, and between 169 and 282 people dead, the worst devastation between Bad Axe and Port Sanilac.

1882 In terms of temperature, it is an exceptionally moderate year: after a winter low of +8° in January, Detroit's high for the summer is only 88°.

A series of six strong tornadoes plows across the countryside from Van Buren to Oakland counties on April 6, killing 10, including a father protecting his family with his own body. Several farms were destroyed by large funnels up to a quarter of a mile wide. The same day another tornado cleared a 3-mile swath of forest near Midland.

1883 June rains total 16.24" at Battle Creek. A half-mile-wide tornado takes three lives—two of them children—on its 15-mile track from Eaton Rapids to Leslie on July 23.

1885 The first day of spring—March 21—brings Detroit its latest zero reading, and the Detroit River remains closed to navigation until April 17.

1886 On April 6, Detroit's deepest 24-hour snowfall—24.5"—brings traffic to a halt. Lakes Michigan and Huron stand 3.2' above the 20th century average in June, 4" higher than the 1986 peak.

1888 This is the sixth and final year of a protracted cool spell with consistently below-normal temperatures across all of Michigan. The cooling had been greatest in the U.P., where Marquette and Escanaba had annual average temperatures 2° to 5° below current normals, while the Lower Peninsula ran 1° to 4° below normal. It is the coldest period of such length in Michigan records.

Marquette is struck by its only tornado on record on August 20. The 50-foot wide twister is described by the Army weather observer as "a dark and heavy mass of cloud shaped like a balloon with fan-like wings [that] hovered nearly over the center of the city for about one minute and then plunged downward." Among the casualties of the tornado are numerous roofs, chimneys, awnings, and a circus tent. The storm also dumps 0.5" of rain and one inch of hail in 5 minutes.

1889 Detroit's driest year: 21.06" of precipitation.

1890 Winter (December-February) averages 35.2° at Detroit, second warmest on record. Despite the warmth, 34.5" snow falls at Marquette, February 25 to March 1. A sustained wind speed of 95 m.p.h. at Detroit in a June thunderstorm is the highest wind ever measured at a major weather station in Michigan.

1894 Lansing has a completely rainless August.

1895 An intense low-pressure system passing over Lansing brings 76 m.p.h. winds to Detroit and gales to all five Great Lakes on November 26.

1896 On May 25, a series of five powerful tornadoes marches eastward from Tuscola, Genesee, and Oakland counties. One tracks 30 miles from the Sterling Heights area into Canada, but the most devastating leaves 47 dead along its half-mile-wide path through Oakwood, Ortonville, and Thomas. It has been estimated that winds exceeded 260 m.p.h. in this killer tornado.

1897 A delightfully warm Easter (April 18) at Marquette turns sour as a cold front sends the mercury plummeting from 60° to 25° between 5:30 and 7:00 P.M. According to the *Mining Journal*, the sudden change "gave even the oldest residents a fuller idea of the depth of total depravity to which Upper Peninsula weather can sink."

1899 The most widespread arctic outbreak in U.S. history sends temperature tumbling below zero from Montana to Florida. In Michigan, Ewen remains below zero for eight consecutive days—February 4 to February 11—bottoming out at -47° on the 10th. Humboldt and Baldwin record -49°, setting state records that hold for 35 years. Local all-time records for cold range from -24° at Battle Creek and Grand Rapids to -43° at Holland.

A 70-pound meteorite thunders across the sky and lands at Thomas Hill on Saugatuck Road, Allegan County, on July 10.

Eight inches of snow fall at Rock in September.

1900 The still vigorous remnants of the Galveston hurricane, which took 6,000 lives along the Texas coast (the greatest disaster in U.S. history), tracks across Michigan on September 11. Winds as high as 72 m.p.h. whipped Lake Michigan, sending many passenger steamers back to port and nearly sinking the ferry *Muskegon*. Thousands of trees loaded with ripe peaches were flattened in southwest Michigan's orchards.

1901 "Buckshot-size" sleet pellets pepper lower Michigan on March 11-12, halting train traffic and downing telegraph wires. On March 24, a waterspout that develops over Indian Lake, near Flint, creates a minor flood when it comes ashore and dumps its load of water. July 15 is Marquette's hottest day ever at 108°.

1903 Temperatures fall to 20° in July at Baraga and Wetmore. Sault Ste. Marie, however, manages to remain just above freezing in July and ends up with its longest freeze-free season ever (170 days).

1904 Michigan's coldest winter of the 20th century (so far) averages 8.4° at Sault Ste. Marie, 18.7° at Detroit, and 13.5° statewide.

1905 At least five people die as a tornado completely wipes out three farms in Sanilac County on June 5.

On July 26 an earthquake centered near Calumet topples chimneys, breaks windows, and sends dishes crashing to floors. It is the strongest of four quakes to rattle the U.P. between 1905 and 1909. (The rash of quakes has been blamed on ore removal near a fault line in the Keweenaw Peninsula.)

In terms of number of ships lost, 1905 is Lake Superior's worst year ever—22 ships sink or are damaged beyond repair, with a total loss of over 30 lives. Severe storms strike on August 31, September 4, October 20, and November 28. Humboldt records Michigan's only subzero October reading, -3°.

1910 Michigan enjoys its warmest and driest March on record. The statewide average of 0.25" precipitation makes it Michigan's driest month on record (since 1895), and at Lapeer the thermometer soars to a record 89°.

Sault Ste. Marie records only 14.6 hours of sunshine in November, a mere 5 percent of possible daylight hours.

1911 A 110° reading at Bay City on July 2 sets a state record that stands for 25 years.

1912 January's *average* temperature is a frigid -7.2° at Watersmeet. There is speculation along the shores of Lake Superior that the lake has frozen over completely, but no one ventures out far enough to verify it.

1913 West winds of 86 m.p.h. whip Detroit on March 21, downing wires and overturning cars. For one hour—10 to 11 A.M.—Detroit's wind averages 71 m.p.h.

The "Freshwater Fury" storm rakes the eastern Great Lakes on November 9 and November 10, sinking eight large vessels on Lake Huron, with a loss of over 200 lives. Winds reach 60 to 90 m.p.h. in the storm, which takes an unusual northward track from Georgia to Lake Huron.

1914 A 9.78" rainstorm at Bloomingdale on September 1 sets a state record for a 24-hour soaking.

1915 A cool summer brings yearly high temperatures of only 89° at Detroit and 86° at Lansing. The state's high, 96° at Seney, comes unusually early—on April 26—while August brings readings as low as 21° at Baraga. The overall statewide summer average of 63.0 sets a record that will stand until 1992.

1917 Coldest year (since 1888), with a statewide average of 40.9°, brings the worst ice conditions on record in northern Great Lakes. Marquette harbor remains closed until May 17. Then a quick heat wave sweeps the state on July 29; Marquette reaches 105°. Late December brings a low of -38° at Humboldt, Michigan's all-time cold record for the last month of the year.

On June 6, a fast-moving (60 m.p.h.) and long-lived (nearly 2 hours) tornado destroys or damages hundreds of farms and homes from the south side of Battle Creek to South Lyon. Four people die and damage exceeds $1 million. (Possibly three tornadoes touched down in sequence, rather than a single funnel.) The same day another tornado forms as a waterspout on Lake Michigan and tracks 10 miles inland after coming ashore south of Grand Haven.

1918 According to the Weather Bureau, "12/26/17 to 1/23/18 was coldest 30 days in Weather Bureau records since 1871." In Michigan the statewide average of 14.6° makes it the second-coldest winter on record, and a widespread flu outbreak and wartime fuel shortages add to the misery. In contrast, summer brings heat that peaks on August 5-6 with temperatures of 108° at Morenci and Plymouth, 104° at Detroit, and 102° at Lansing.

1919 A deep low pressure center drops the barometer to 28.21" at Sault Ste. Marie on Nov. 29, and brings sustained winds reaching 67 m.p.h. at Detroit and 59 m.p.h. at Port Huron.

1920 Numerous tornadoes—possibly 14 or more—ravage southern and western counties of the Lower Peninsula on March 28. The onslaught lasts 7 hours; 14 people die, and damage reaches $2 million. Lansing's low for the winter of 1920-21 is a relatively mild +3° in December.

1921 An exceptionally mild winter, spring, and summer (which doesn't leave much left, and only October and November are near normal) make 1921 Michigan's warmest year on record (since 1888), with a statewide average of 48.3°. Detroit's low for the year is a mild 9°. Over an inch of freezing rain coats Alpena, December 16-17.

1922 Michigan's worst ice storm glazes an east-west belt, 50 to 100 miles wide, with up to 2" of ice from February 21 to 23. One foot of coated telephone wire weighed 11 pounds!

1923 Detroit enjoys its third winter in a row without below-zero temperatures, although Humboldt manages a reading of -46° on February 5. An April cold wave sends temperatures below zero as far south as the middle of the lower peninsula, with Bergland reaching -34°. Sault Ste. Marie records its earliest measurable snow, 0.3" on September 13.

1924 October averages only 0.48" of rain across the state, its driest October in history.

1925 A total solar eclipse sweeps across northern Michigan on the morning of January 24, but, sadly, clouds obscure the view. Observers have better luck in Minnesota and New York.

A snowstorm October 25-27 is followed by temperatures as low as +2° at Ironwood.

Sault Ste. Marie is totally socked-in the first 15 days of December—not a minute of sunshine recorded—but despite the clouds, it is the driest year ever at Sault Ste. Marie (20.69") and Alpena (17.41").

1926 As a result of the recent dry weather, Lake Superior drops to 1.8' below normal in April, its lowest level on record.

1927 The barometer rises to 31.15" at Sault Ste. Marie on January 26, a record high for Michigan. The Canadian freighter *Kamloops* runs into heavy snow, hurricane-force winds, and freezing spray off Isle Royale on December 6. The weight of the ice topples the smokestack, and the ship loses power and sinks; all 33 on board die.

1928 An ice storm covers the entire U.P. with glaze, April 6-7.

1929 May snowfall records ranging from 2.5" at Gull Lake to 13" at Atlanta result from snowstorms May 2-3 and May 15-16. A strong undertow on Lake Michigan, caused by brisk southwest winds, sweeps nine people to their deaths at Grand Haven on July 4. An autumn snowburst dumps 27" of snow on Ishpeming in 24 hours on October 23.

1930 Statewide precipitation of 22.31" makes this Michigan's driest year on record (since 1888), and it is also the driest at Grand Rapids, Lansing, and Muskegon.

1931 The state's low for the winter of 1930-31 is a mere -21°, the mildest winter low on record. Statewide, it is the second-warmest year on record, while Sault Ste. Marie records the warmest year (44.3°) in its 170-year weather history. Autumn (September-November) averages 53.2° statewide, another warm record, and Christmas brings a thunderstorm with hail at Lansing.

1932 Michigan enjoys another mild winter, with the state's low being -22° at Sidnaw. The statewide average of 28.7° for December-February is 7° above normal, and this is the warmest winter since 1895. Detroit's 35.6° average makes it the warmest winter since 1840! The warm weather brings a rare February tornado to Owosso.

1933 Michigan's only January tornado on record touches down near Britton. A three-year warm spell can't quite make it through another year—the temperature plunges to -37° near Vanderbilt on December 29.

1934 An overnight low of -51° at Pigeon River Forest (near Vanderbilt) on February 8 is the coldest on record in Michigan; at Sault Ste. Marie the daily range from 37° to -12° makes it their coldest day ever. Less than 4 months later (on June 1), Vanderbilt swelters at 105°.

A May thunderstorm whips Marquette with a sustained 91 m.p.h. wind. On Memorial Day a heat wave reaches 100° in the U.P., and the next day 107° heat at Houghton Lake sets an all-time record there and a June record for the state. One-inch hail falls on Sault Ste. Marie, June 29.

1935 Michigan narrowly misses another severe cold wave on January 23, as an arctic high-pressure system settles over Ontario. The mercury dips to -40° at Sidnaw, but 240 miles northeast of Sault Ste. Marie, at the center of the high, Iroquois Falls (Ontario) records -73°, the coldest ever seen in North America outside of Alaska and the Yukon.

An earthquake on November 1 shakes Sault Ste. Marie and puts several new cracks in the walls of the downtown weather bureau office.

1936 It is a year of extremes: Bessemer records 35 consecutive nights with temperatures reaching 0° or lower from January 19 to February 22, including a stretch of four days with afternoons remaining below zero (January 22-25). Summer brings a record heat wave that bakes Kalamazoo with 101° to 109° readings on nine consecutive days, July 7-15. After a winter low of -34°, Mio records an all-time state heat record of 112° on July 13. Only Muskegon and Whitefish Point escape the heat, with summer highs of 89° and 88°, respectively. Just 15.64" of precipitation fall on Croswell all year, the lowest yearly total in Michigan history. The drought drops the levels of Lakes Erie and St. Clair to 3' below normal.

1938 A 36-hour blizzard on January 24-26 buries Marquette under 18" of snow whipped by 60-m.p.h. winds into drifts 20' to 30' high. Snowplows bogged down in the dense drifts have to be excavated by shovel-wielding humans.

1939 Heaviest March snow ever at Marquette drops 16" in 24 hours of the 14th and 15th. A month later, on April 17 and 18, Marquette is glazed by 0.5" to 1" of freezing rain.

Two tornado swarms—five on June 10, and four on August 8—rake the southern half of the Lower Peninsula. Tornadoes destroy houses near Kalamazoo on both dates, and the August storm kills two in the southeastern part of Kalamazoo.

Around 8 A.M. on June 18 a heavy thunderstorm triggers a seiche on Lake Superior that inundates docks and reverses flowing creeks from L'Anse to Munising. Six-foot fluctuations continue at half-hour intervals well into the afternoon.

Double trouble strikes Marquette on Sunday, September 3. The first storm, at 11:15 A.M., brings walnut-sized hail that smashes windows and greenhouses across town, along with high winds that swamp boats on Lake Superior. The second storm two hours later dumps 1.4" of rain in 20 minutes, washing out roads and flooding basements, and sinks another boat, drowning a man who has gone out to rescue three fishermen lost in the earlier storm.

1940 The great "Armistice Day Storm" comes out of the Pacific Ocean, cuts across Oklahoma, and tracks northward across western Lake Superior, creating all sorts of havoc. Three large ships and several small craft go down on Lake Michigan, with a total loss of 69 lives. On the afternoon of November 11 a severe squall line associated with the storm crosses lower Michigan in less than three hours, bringing peaks winds of 80 m.p.h. to Grand Rapids and 61 m.p.h. at Alpena. Lansing Shoal Light, at the north end of Lake Michigan, reports gusts to 100 m.p.h., and Houghton's barometer bottoms out at 28.57".

Averaged across the state, 1940 has the most cloudy days (164) and fewest clear days (104) of any year in the 1888-1947 period during which such averages were computed. It is also the snowiest year during the same period, with a statewide average of 82.7".

1942 An intense low sends the barometer to 28.60" at Alpena on March 9.

1943 Isle Royale's coldest day, -29°, is March 2. Early fall brings killing frosts on September 11 and 24 to much of Michigan; Ann Arbor's earliest measurable snow falls on October 16.

1944 Sault Ste. Marie's latest first snow falls on November 20. It totals 1".

1945 Michigan's biggest June snowstorm ever leaves a trace at Sault Ste. Marie, 2" at Calumet, and 7" at Ishpeming on the 2nd.

1946 Seiches develop on Lakes Superior, Michigan, Huron, and Erie on June 16 as a line of thunderstorms moves southeastward across the lakes. The lakes rise and fall as much as 2' at Marquette, Sault Ste. Marie, and Port Huron, and at some locations the up-and-down oscillations continue for 12 to 24 hours. The next day, a tornado touches down south of Detroit, injuring 35 people; crossing into Windsor, Ontario, it kills 15 (making it one of Canada's deadliest tornadoes). On June 27 another tornado crosses from Windsor to downtown Detroit, where it damages a bus garage.

1947 August averages a steamy 81.9 degrees at Dowagiac.

1949 Only 1.1" snow falls at Eaton Rapids during the winter of 1948-49. This is also the least-snowy winter on record at Champion, but their total was 81.5".

1950 The winter of 1949-50 is Michigan's wettest since 1895, with a December-February total of 8.94" of precipitation statewide. The wet winter is highlighted by the state's snowiest single storm: 46.1" at Calumet, January 15-20. That same month Millington measures no snow whatsoever. Warm weather invades the state in late January, bringing Sault Ste. Marie its first January thunderstorm in 34 years on the 24th. The next day, temperatures soar to 72° at Ann Arbor, Michigan's warmest January day ever.

A northwest wind of 93 m.p.h. on June 25 is the highest sustained speed ever reported by a ship on Lake Superior.

An early freeze on August 22 closes out Sault Ste. Marie's shortest growing season ever—98 days. On September 24, northwesterly winds carry a dense smoke cloud from burning forests in western Canada across eastern Michigan, darkening the skies at mid-afternoon. Birds and chickens go to roost and outdoor lights have to be turned on. There are reports of blue moons and even a bluish sun seen through the smoke.

November brings an amazing range of temperatures—the month opens with a summerlike 84° at Wayne, and closes with -23° at Pellston around Thanksgiving.

1951 Snow falls for 53 consecutive days at Houghton, ending January 8.

1952 On May 5, northwest winds lift Lake Huron 5' at Port Huron; the subsequent seiche at the other end of the lake floods Portage Street in Sault Ste. Marie when the Soo Locks overflow.

1953 This is by far Michigan's worst year ever for tornadoes. The year's total of 13 tornadoes is not exceptional, but six of those are killers. On May 21, a 3,000-foot-wide tornado kills two people and destroys 90 homes in Port Huron before crossing the border to Sarnia, Ontario, where four others die. On June 8, killer tornadoes strike near Ypsilanti and Tawas City, and another tornado kills four near Erie before heading out across Lake Erie. It almost reaches the other side of the lake near Kingsville, Ontario, before it dissipates. At 8:30 P.M. the worst tornado of the lot strikes just north of Flint, leaving 115 dead and 844 injured in its wake. That tornado lifts near Lapeer, but another takes its place and continues across northern St. Clair County. The total toll for the day is 125 dead, nearly 1,000 injured, and $19 million of damage.

Another deadly storm on May 10-11 whips Lake Superior with winds to 60 m.p.h., sending the freighter *Henry Steinbrenner* to the bottom with its 17-man crew.

1954 At 24.4°, February is the warmest on record at Sault Ste. Marie.

A deadly seiche swamps Montrose Harbor in Chicago on June 26, drowning 7 as they fish from a pier. The seiche developed as thunderstorm winds piled water up against the Michigan shore of Lake Michigan, and the water sloshed back to Illinois after the storms moved inland.

1955 Detroit records its hottest month (July, 79.1°) and summer (June-August, 74.4°) in history. This is also Sault Ste. Marie's hottest summer (67.2°), and Wayne's average daily high temperature in July is a sizzling 92.4°.

1956 It is another devastating tornado year. On April 3, the first and worst of the deadly tornadoes leaves 18 dead along its 65-mile track from Saugatuck to Trufant, with the worst damage in Hudsonville and west side of Grand Rapids. A total of 332 homes are ruined. At about the same time, another tornado comes off Lake Michigan near Portage Point and tracks northeast into Grand Traverse Bay and, 40 minutes later, yet another twister strikes near Allegan. Nineteen tornadoes strike the central and southeastern counties of the Lower Peninsula on May 12-13. A near miss occurs at 5:06 A.M. on May 13 as the tip of a funnel cloud passes barely 100' above the Weather Bureau office at Muskegon.

It is a very cool, wet July at Sault Ste. Marie: the high for the month is only 78°, and a record 6.04" of rain falls. Another record—2.7" of snow—falls at Sault Ste. Marie in September.

1958 The highest temperature that Michigan could muster all summer is only 95° on August 9, at an odd place—Huron Mountain, in Marquette County.

On November 18 the freighter *Carl D. Bradley*, for many years the largest ship on the Great lakes, breaks up in 65 m.p.h. winds and 20-foot waves near Beaver Island, Lake Michigan, and goes down with her crew of 33. The southwesterly gales were a result of a cyclone tracking northward across Minnesota.

1959 The coldest winter in 23 years freezes the ground up to 6' deep in parts of the state. Sault Ste. Marie accumulates 40" of snow on the ground by March 16. October is a dull one for sunshine: the 39 hours of sunshine at Alpena make up only 11 percent of possible daylight hours.

1960 A one-day total of 33.5" of snow belts Baldwin on November 30.

1961 The remnants of Hurricane Carla, which stormed ashore at Port Lavaca, Texas, on September 11, cross Michigan on the morning of the 14th. Three to six inches of rain drench an area from Eau Claire to Cheboygan, washing out two dams on the Boardman River, while a small tornado damages farm buildings near Traverse City. September rainfall totals of 12.49" at Eau Claire, 9.48" at Boyne Falls, and 9.36" at Onaway make it the wettest month ever at those locations.

1962 A cloudburst dumps 1.46" of rain on Detroit in just five minutes on August 4.

1963 Watersmeet and Ironwood remain below zero for five consecutive days, January 19-23. By late February, Lake Superior has iced over except for patches no larger than an acre or two.

With only 0.16" of rain, it is the driest October on record at Sault Ste. Marie.

About 25 waterspouts are sighted in Traverse Bay between 11 A.M. and noon on October 28. Those that come ashore dissipate immediately, although golf-ball–size hail falls as one spout makes landfall. Lake-effect snows total 82.6" at Muskegon in December, with a peak accumulation of 34" on the 20th.

1964 Lake Michigan bottoms out at 2.5' below normal levels in March, the lowest the lake has been in recorded history.

Severe weather strikes all of lower Michigan on May 8, the worst storm being a tornado north of Mt. Clemens that kills 11 and demolishes 132 homes.

Two people are killed and four injured at Detroit by a single lightning strike in August.

At Houghton Lake, this is the last of 13 consecutive years without a freeze in July or August.

Muskegon reaches 99° on August 3, setting a new high temperature record for both August and all time. Six days later, a 40° reading sets a new *low* temperature record for August.

October is one of the driest months on record across most of the Midwest, including Michigan.

1965 Ten inches of snow paralyze Detroit on February 25.

March is a dreary month across lower Michigan, with only 94 hours of sunshine at Grand Rapids. The warmest anywhere in the state is only 54° at Benton Harbor.

A massive tornado outbreak on Palm Sunday (April 11) unleashes at least 37 tornadoes from Iowa to Ohio. In 11 hours, 257 people died, including 53 in southern Michigan, and over 3,000 were hurt. Of the 16 tornadoes in Michigan, the largest cut a 90-mile-long, 6,000-foot-wide path from Lake Pleasant (Indiana) to sites near Waltz, Wayne County.

A ship measures winds of 109 m.p.h. during a squall on Lake Huron on August 6, the highest wind reported by a ship on the Lakes.

1966 An early May cold snap sends the mercury to 8° at Vanderbilt.

On August 3, a dust devil in Saginaw picks up a doghouse (with dog) and drops it in the neighbor's yard. Fortunately, the dog is unhurt.

Lansing records its earliest freeze on September 16.

Winds reaching 75 m.p.h. sweep all of Michigan on November 27-28, causing widespread damage in lower Michigan and whipping up a blizzard in the Upper Peninsula. The ore carrier *Daniel C. Morell* breaks in two on Lake Huron near Harbor Beach, and all but one of its 29-man crew are lost.

Novembers are usually cloudy in Michigan, but this year is an extreme; the November sun shines on Sault Ste. Marie for only 24 hours (8 percent of possible hours).

1967 Fifteen to 30 inches of snow clobber an 80-mile-wide band from Benton Harbor to Flint on January 26-27, collapsing roofs and closing schools for as long as a week. Lansing's 24" is its greatest snowfall ever, and classes at Michigan State University are canceled for the first time in its 112-year history.

Six hours of 30- to 50-m.p.h. winds (gusting as high as 85 m.p.h.) following a cold front passage on February 16 start a seiche on Lake Erie that causes the water level to rise 8' at Buffalo, New York, and fall 7' at Monroe. Lake levels continue to oscillate for two days after the winds cease. The high winds blow out picture windows all across the southern half of lower Michigan.

Ten tornadoes sweep southern Michigan on April 21, the worst of which destroys 65 buildings and damages 435 along its 20-mile-wide path from Grandville to Ada in Kent County. Four days later, one of the tornado's lesser cousins, a dust devil, drops out of a clear sky and topples a trailer in northeast Detroit.

On July 18, 15 minutes worth of golf-ball–sized hail piles 15" deep in a square mile area near Battle Creek, flattening all sorts of vegetables. The next day, 4.55" of rain falls in one hour at Royal Oak.

High winds and 6' to 10' seas swamp numerous fishing boats near Frankfort on September 23, drowning seven people.

Six to ten inches of wet, heavy snow plaster much of southern Michigan on October 27, downing trees and wires and setting early-season records at Muskegon, Lansing, and Grand Rapids.

1968 On March 13, gale-force winds shove pack ice as far as 400' inland at Bay City State Park on Saginaw Bay, crushing trees and picnic tables.

A rare clockwise-rotating tornado damages 100 buildings at Maybee, Monroe County, on March 26. The tornado formed along the "cold front" at the leading edge of a lake breeze.

Six children are hurt on June 7 when lightning strikes an antenna and blows up a television set at a home in Cement City.

A seiche in the Keweenaw Bay on June 30 causes the lake to rise four times between 11 A.M. and 5:30 P.M. The greatest rise, 6' above normal, inundates highway M41 between Baraga and L'Anse and floods some basements in the area.

Two storms two hours apart pile hail 21" deep near Shepherd, Isabella County, on July 5. Another storm the same day dumps 24" of hail (in drifts) near Yale, St. Clair County.

A brilliant midday meteor streaks from north to south above Grand Rapids on August 27, rattling the city with several sonic booms.

Michigan is rattled again on November 9, this time by a 5.5 Richter magnitude earthquake centered in southern Illinois. The quake shakes a total of 20 states from Georgia to Minnesota, but no damage is reported.

1969 A dry February brings only 0.44" of precipitation, averaged across Michigan.

Only two days after a frosty 32° morning, Marquette soars to 100.2° on May 28, a local record for May and the state's highest reading all year.

Sault Ste. Marie records its latest spring freeze ever on June 21.

Viewers at East Lansing see a bright green meteor pass directly in front of the moon around midnight on June 26.

A severe squall line on the Fourth of July whips western Lake Michigan with sustained winds of 100 m.p.h.—the highest ever measured by a ship on the lake. The skies are alive over southwestern Michigan on July 28, with 75 funnel clouds sighted between noon and 10:30 P.M. Most of the funnels are seen near Grand Rapids, and none of them touches the ground.

Several waterspouts are seen over Lake Michigan near Charlevoix and Shelby on October 22 as the air temperature stands near freezing.

1970 January lake-effect snows, most resulting from three arctic outbreaks, total 60" at Muskegon. Across Lake Michigan, Milwaukee receives only 6" for the month. A record April snowstorm, accompanied by lightning, dumps 17" on Lansing on the 1st.

A series of electrical storms rakes the Detroit metro area during the night of May 22-23, setting fires that destroy or damage five barns and five homes. The lightning that set the $5 million blaze at the Swedish Crucible Steel Co. in Hamtramck went down in the books as Michigan's most damaging lightning strike ever.

1971 By February 16, snow has accumulated to 80" on the ground at Marquette Airport, the greatest snow depth ever measured in Michigan.

1972 Sault Ste. Marie's winter snowfall, 172.4", breaks the record of 144" established the previous winter! A 50" snow depth on March 7 is also a record, and on March 9 Munising has 76" on the ground. Lake Superior is reported to be 95 percent ice-covered. Lansing has its latest freezing temperature, 32°, on June 11. Sixty to 90 percent of the blueberry crop is lost in some areas.

Strong easterly winds on November 14 raise the waters of western Lakes Huron and Erie by 5' to 7', flooding extensive areas of lowlands and forcing the evacuation of 8,000 residents. The worst flooding is in Bay and Monroe counties.

1973 On March 16-18, strong northeast winds once again push the waters of Saginaw Bay up to five miles inland. This time, evacuations are hampered by 20" of snow that falls in the same storm.

A squall line on June 26 whips Detroit Metropolitan Airport with 87 m.p.h. sustained winds and 94 m.p.h. gusts.

1974 Michigan has 39 tornadoes, the most ever in one year. Among the twisters is Michigan's second-ever February tornado, which destroys a shed near New Boston (Wayne Co.) on the 28th. While five tornadoes strike southern Michigan on the evening of April 3, freezing rain and up to a foot of snow fall on the Upper Peninsula. Another tornado on July 14 empties the water out of a swimming pool near Mt. Clemens, but does little damage otherwise.

December 1 brings Ann Arbor its greatest one-day snowfall, 15.8".

1975 Hailstones as large as 3" break windows in 5,000 homes and 5,000 cars and destroy 10 greenhouses near Holland on June 4.

At least six lightning strikes on August 23 land in the middle of the Wheel Inn Campground near Lansing, injuring 90 of the 500 people at a campers' convention.

A November gale rakes all of Michigan with 60 m.p.h. winds on the 10th, downing trees, signs, and antennas. Winds reach 71 m.p.h. at Sault Ste. Marie and are probably higher over Lake Superior, where, at 7:25 P.M., the ore carrier *Edmund Fitzgerald* goes down with all 29 crewmen. The same storm brings a small tornado to Allegan County.

1976 On February 27, 71° at Benton Harbor sets a state record for the month.

On March 3, a day of freezing rain leaves up to 1.5" of clear ice in a 70-mile-wide swatch from Muskegon to Port Sanilac (including the northern suburbs of Detroit), downing power lines, trees, and roofs. Electric power is knocked out in 600,000 homes, including 90 percent of Saginaw; Saginaw County is declared a disaster area. In some towns, nearly every tree is damaged or destroyed, and fruit orchards are devastated. The next day, more freezing rain— up to 0.5"—causes similar problems in a seven-county area just north of the area hit by the previous storm; meanwhile, a tornado leaves a 43-mile-long trail of fallen trees in Berrien and Van Buren counties. Three major tornado outbreaks during March—7 in southwest Michigan on the 12th, 5 in south central and southeastern counties on the 20th, and 5 more north of Saginaw Bay on the 30th—push the month's tornado total to 18.

Autumn is the coldest on record, with a statewide September-November average of 43.4°. It is also dry across the Upper Peninsula—from June 1 through the end of the year, Marquette receives only 10.68" of precipitation (half the normal amount), leading to water shortages and dry wells the following winter.

1977 A bitterly cold January averages -1.2° at Ironwood, while the average daily minimum is -12.9° at Bergland and Crystal Falls, and the lowest -42° at Stambaugh. The warmest anywhere in the state for the entire month is a humble 36°. The ground freezes to a depth of 3' to 5' over much of the state, and wells freeze solid in the Ontonagon area.

For the third time in six years, Sault Ste. Marie sets a new seasonal snow record: 178.6" for winter 1976-77. Grand Marais measures 282.3" and Tahquamenon Falls has 332.8"—both all-time records—while Saginaw's 16.4" is the *least* on record there!

Michigan's third-coldest winter since 1895 (December-February average 14.8°) comes to a sudden halt in late February, and is followed by the warmest spring on record (March-May average 47.7°). May is exceptionally sunny, with Alpena, Detroit, Lansing, Marquette, and Sault Ste. Marie all recording more 300 hours of sunshine, or 80 to 85 percent of all daylight hours. Summer is cooler than normal, but a hot blast sears Marquette on July 19 with 104°.

1978 The "Blizzard of '78" whips all of Michigan with 1' to 2' of snow and 50 to 70 m.p.h. winds on January 26. Drifts as high as 50' brought all traffic to a standstill, and 120,000 vehicles were abandoned in the snow. The low pressure responsible for the storm produced a barometer reading of 28.21" at Port Huron.

Hail up to 3.5" across shatters windows and punctures roofs near Munising on July 19.

High winds capsizes the paddlewheeler *Mark Twain* on Lake St. Clair on November 17.

1979 Delaware, on the Keweenaw Peninsula, has 56.4" of snow in 12 days, January 19-30. The 1978-79 seasonal total at Delaware, 391.9", is the most ever measured in one winter in Michigan. Sault Ste. Marie averaged -1.7° for first 19 days of February, bottoming out at -35° on 17th. At the end of the cold spell, the Coast Guard announces that Lake Superior was completely frozen over (except for a few "fingers") for the first time since 1963. The ice ranged from 6" to 25" thick.

The state's highest temperature for the year is only 94°, reached at Lapeer in June and Grosse Pointe and Monroe in August. This is Michigan's lowest annual high since at least 1888.

Forty-five National Guardsmen are injured slightly on June 20 when lightning strikes the antenna at their radio tent at Camp Grayling, Crawford County.

A dry September: 12 locations in the Lower Peninsula receive no rain at all, and 16 more locations receive only a sprinkle.

1980 A 1,400-foot-wide tornado rips through the center of Kalamazoo on May 13, destroying or damaging over 1,000 houses and leaving 5 people dead, 79 injured, and 1,200 homeless. A nearly instantaneous pressure drop of 0.59" is recorded on a barometer at the American Bank in Kalamazoo as the tornado passes overhead. Another tornado in Van Buren County 30 minutes earlier left 700 homeless.

On May 30, a squall line brings high winds, funnel clouds, and a small tornado to southwestern lower Michigan. Winds reach 115 m.p.h. at the St. Joseph Coast Guard Station.

Powerful thunderstorms pummel a swath from St. Joseph to southern Wayne County on the morning of July 16, wrecking innumerable buildings and vehicles with winds estimated as high as 150 m.p.h. Nineteen people are injured and a boy is killed by falling trees. Damage reaches $100 million.

A record 69.3" of snow buries Sault Ste. Marie in December.

1982 A bitter January brings record cold and snow to much of Michigan. Hurricane force gusts and below-zero temperatures produce wind chills of -50° to -80° on the 10th. Over a foot of lake-effect snow at Sleeping Bear Dunes triggers an avalanche that injures four skiers. Another cold wave a week later sends the temperature to -41° at Ironwood; the daytime maximum of -21° on the 17th is the coldest day ever recorded in Michigan. The January snow total of 71" at Sault Ste. Marie is the most ever measured there in a single month.

Summer is cold, too, averaging 2.6° below normal across the state.

Up to 10.63" of rain falls near Holland on the night of July 16-17, submerging some roads under 5' of water and washing out several highways.

Hailstones 3.5" in diameter shatter a greenhouse in Baraga County on August 2. Early morning record temperatures above 60° at Detroit, Lansing, and Grand Rapids on December 28 are replaced by wind gusts in the 60s as a cold front passed.

1983 On May 2, a tornado touches down in East Detroit, moves northeast across Lake St. Clair as a "thick black waterspout," strikes Harsens Island, and moves into Canada. Dozens of homes, several boats, and an airplane hanger are destroyed.

A long, warm summer boosts the water temperature in the Sault Ste. Marie power canal to a record 72° on August 7-8 and September 4-6. On August 8, the thermometer reached an all-time high of 94° at Mott Island, Isle Royale.

1984 On July 23, ball lightning—mysterious glowing blobs ever so rarely observed during thunderstorms—roll across a field near Sidney and strike a boy, killing him.

1985 The wettest year statewide since 1888 has an average 39.56" of precipitation. The Great Lakes respond by rising to their highest levels in a century; in October, Lake Superior peaks at 1.3' above the 20th century's average.

On New Year's Day, 1" of freezing rain falls on top of 2" to 5" of new snow along a 50-mile-wide area from South Haven to Lansing to Lakeport. Power is knocked out to 404,000 customers for up to 10 days.

On June 8, a small tornado topples a tree onto a tent at Shakey Lakes County Park in Menominee County, killing a man inside the tent. He is the Upper Peninsula's first known tornado fatality.

A six-hour downpour dumps 12.24" of rain on the northern parts of Flint on the morning of September 6, damaging 100,000 buildings with flood water.

High winds on December 1-2 cause lakeshore flooding that damages homes and highways around Keweenaw Bay and washes four houses into Lake Michigan; Lake Erie drops 8' at Monroe as the wind-pushed lake water rises an unprecedented 12' at Buffalo, New York, creating a 20-foot difference across the lake! The storm dumped 36.4" of snow on Marquette.

1986 March 8-10, Sault Ste. Marie receives 14.8" snow along with thunder, freezing rain, and sleet.

A thunderstorm dumps 6.72" rain on De Tour Village, July 5.

Sault Ste. Marie records its first August snow ever—a trace—on the 27th, while a brief showers of snow pellets pelts Negaunee and Gwinn in the hills above Marquette.

Lakes Erie and St. Clair reach record levels of 2.5' above normal in June and July.

Two days of thunderstorms across central lower Michigan culminate with a record-setting downpour on the morning of September 11. The storm total of 13.47" at Big Rapids sets a state record, as does the monthly total of 19.26" at Edmore. Flooding in a 60-mile-wide strip from Muskegon to Port Sanilac also sets a state damage record of $400 million. The deluge pushes Lakes Michigan and Huron to 3.2' above average in October, a rise of 6.3' since 1964 and the highest in 100 years.

1987 A lake-effect "snowburst" dumps 27.5" of snow on Munising on April 1-2, burying cars in 6-foot drifts. Less than 40 miles away at Grand Marais, only 1" of snow falls. As the storm gears up on the afternoon of the 1st, a brief tornado drops out of a snow squall and damages a mobile home on the south shore of Whitefish Bay. At many other locations in the

U.P., the winter of 1986-87 has the least snow in 29 years. Included is Toivola, where "only" 165.3" is the least on record!

On July 9, a tornado passing east of Munising strikes a commercial dog kennel, picking up one of its residents and depositing him unharmed in a treetop half a mile away.

Saginaw's 105° on July 21 is Michigan's hottest day in 51 years.

1988 A long, hot summer brings 106° heat to Monroe on June 26 (Michigan's hottest day in 52 years) and unpleasant 82° overnight lows to Holland and South Haven on August 17. The persistent heat raises the water temperature of western Lake Erie to 86° (about as warm as the Caribbean in summer) on August 2, 1988.

It is also a dry summer, statewide average rainfall reaching record lows in May (1.09") and June (.95").

1989 On March 27, Sault Ste. Marie records a high temperature of 60° followed by 1.5" hailstones—all this with 18" of snow on the ground! December dumps 129.3" of snow on Delaware, on the Keweenaw Peninsula.

1991 Jagged, baseball-sized hailstones pound a 10-mile-wide area between Ida and Monroe on March 27. At appropriately-named Stony Point, northeast of Monroe, hailstones were measured at 4" in diameter.

1992 Michigan's "Year Without a Summer" averages a whopping 4° below normal, and is the coldest summer since statewide records began in 1895. The hottest all summer anywhere in Michigan is 95° at Grand Rapids. At Sault Ste. Marie, where records extend back to 1823, July's 57.2° is the coldest ever and the month's maximum is only 79°.

On the evening of July 19 a tornado rips through the north side of Gladstone, uprooting trees and flipping cars. An empty 20,000-gallon tank is tossed 200 yards into a larger tank, breaking it open and unleashing its contents—250,000 gallons of tar.

LAKES MICHIGAN & HURON LEVELS
Yearly departures from 92-year average

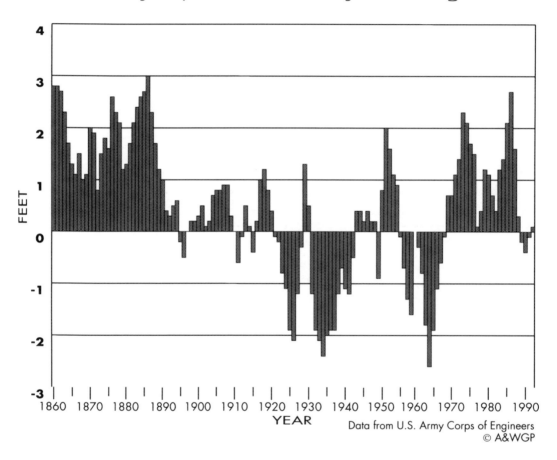

Data from U.S. Army Corps of Engineers
© A&WGP

RESOURCES

■■■■■■■■■■■■■■■■■■■■■■■■■■■

I certainly hope that *Michigan Weather* has whetted—but not completely satisfied—your interest in the weather. If you're still hungry, here's some suggestions about where to go next:

BOOKS

There's no shortage of books about weather, and there's no way I could list them all (or you could buy them all!). I suggest rummaging through the weather shelf at your nearest library and seeing what grabs your fancy. However, I can't resist making a few recommendations:

Weather, by Lehr, Burnett, and Zim, Golden Press, New York. The first edition of this popular little volume appeared in 1957 and it has been updated several times since. It's compact but comprehensive, easy to read and well illustrated, and I have recommended it to audiences from Cub Scouts to mountain climbers. The 1957 edition was my first weather book!

A treasure trove of maps of Michigan's climate can be found in *The Climatic Atlas of Michigan* by Eichenlaub, Harman, Nurnberger, and Stolle (1990, University of Notre Dame Press, Notre Dame, IN 46556). At $49.95 it's more likely to end up in reference libraries than on your coffee table, but maybe if you tell Santa that you've been good all year....

Val Eichenlaub's *Weather and Climate of the Great Lakes Region* (University of Notre Dame Press, 1978) is, unfortunately, out of print, but is well worth the trip to your library if *Michigan Weather* leaves you hungry for more.

Anyone intrigued by maritime weather at its worst should read *Shipwrecks of Lake Superior*, edited by James Marshall and published by *Lake Superior Magazine*, P.O. Box 16417, Duluth, MN 55816-6417, or *Lake Superior Shipwrecks*, by Julius Wolff, Jr., available from the Lake Superior Marine Museum Association, P.O. Box 177, Duluth, MN 55801-0177.

If tornadoes are your cup of tea, *Significant Tornadoes, 1880-1991* (available from: Tornado Project, Box 302, St. Johnsbury, VT 05189) contains facts, descriptions, and photos of literally thousands of tornadoes over the past century. They also have a blockbuster video, "Tornado Video Classics."

Superbly detailed books about weather history and events in Michigan and the rest of the United States are David M. Ludlum's series, *Early American Winters* (Volumes I and II) and

Early American Tornadoes, along with his *The American Weather Book*. All are available from the American Meteorological Society (A.M.S.), 45 Beacon Street, Boston, MA 02108.

The A.M.S. also sells the *International Cloud Atlas, Volume II*, a must for serious cloud watchers. Published in 1987 by the World Meteorological Organization, this lavish (and expensive—$82) volume contains over 200 photographs of clouds and other weather phenomena and is the international standard for identifying cloud types. Much more affordable are the cloud charts (and assorted teaching aids) from How the Weatherworks, 1522 Baylor Avenue, Rockville, MD 20850, and For Spacious Skies, 54 Webb Street, Lexington, MA 02173.

Between these extremes, for $18 you can get T*he Audubon Society Field Guide to North American Weather* (Alfred Knopf, New York, 1991), which has a spectacular selection of photographs.

Finally, if you're curious about the weather of other parts of the country, I can't resist recommending *Skywatch: the Western Weather Guide* and *Skywatch: the Eastern Weather Guide*, by Richard A. Keen, published by Fulcrum, 350 Indiana Street, Suite 350, Golden, CO 80401, and *Minnesota Weather*, also by Richard A. Keen, published by American & World Geographic Publishing, P.O. Box 5630, Helena, MT 59604

PERIODICALS

Weatherwise, published six times a year by Heldref Publications, 4000 Albemarle Street N.W., Washington, DC 20016. For over 40 years this has been the only magazine in America devoted solely to weather. Its articles cover weather research, history, and recent weather events.

Science News reports on the latest discoveries in all the sciences, including meteorology. It's published weekly by Science Service, 231 West Center Street, Marion, Ohio 43305.

American Weather Observer is a monthly tabloid that lists weather reports from amateur weather watchers around the country, including your own, if you wish. Write to the Association of American Weather Observers, P.O. Box 455, 401 Whitney Blvd., Belvidere, IL 61008.

A must for heavy weather addicts is *Storm Track*, a bimonthly newsletter for storm chasers and watchers published by Tim Marshall, 1336 Brazos Blvd., Lewisville, TX 75067, for $10 a year. It's informal and enthusiastic, and features a cartoon called "Funnel Funny!"

The National Weather Association, 4400 Stamp Road, Room 404, Temple Hills, MD 20748, publishes the *National Weather Digest* along with slide sets and a manual for interpreting weather satellite pictures. Articles in the *Digest* are written by real live weather forecasters about specific weather events, and lend an appreciation for what these people do for a living.

The *Bulletin of the American Meteorological Society* is directed to the professional meteorologist, but amateurs will enjoy many of the articles and news notes. It's free to A.M.S. members but quite expensive otherwise (that's what libraries are for). The Society's address is: 45 Beacon St., Boston, MA 02108.

Four times a year *Mariners Weather Log* comes out with articles on the weather of the oceans and Great Lakes. There's even practical advice like how to dodge waterspouts approaching your boat! It's $6 a year from the Superintendent of Documents (see U.S. government publications below), and you can get a free sample copy from National Oceanographic Data Center, NOAA/NESDIS E/OC21, Universal Building, Room 412, Washington, DC 20235.

U.S. GOVERNMENT PUBLICATIONS

The federal government also publishes a variety of reasonably-priced climate- and weather-related publications. The Superintendent of Documents, U.S. Government Printing Office, Washington, DC 20402 has a general catalog, a special catalog of weather-related publications (ask for "Subject Bibliography #234—Weather"), and a monthly listing of new books.

The National Climatic Data Center, Federal Building, Asheville, NC 28801-2696 publishes tons of climate data for all sorts of locations. Write for their free list of "Selected Climatological Publications." Among these are:

Storm Data describes hundreds of storms, from hurricanes to dust devils, that strike the U.S.A. each month. There are maps, photos, and statistics—a bonanza for storm lovers!

Local Climatological Data—Monthly summaries of daily and hourly weather, available for nine cities in Michigan: Alpena, Detroit, Flint, Grand Rapids, Houghton Lake, Lansing, Marquette, Muskegon, and Sault Ste. Marie.

Climatological Data, Michigan—Monthly summaries of temperature, rainfall, snow, and other weather data at dozens of cities and towns from Monroe to Ironwood.

Climates of the States: Michigan. Published for each state of the Union, these informative booklets describe the state's climate in words, numbers, and maps. They include several pages of tabulated statistics about temperature, wind, snow, and the like for selected cities.

The Department of Agriculture, in cooperation with NOAA, puts out a *Weekly Weather and Crop Bulletin* that reports on weather conditions across the nation and around the world, with emphasis on agricultural impacts. It has been published weekly since 1872. Write NOAA/USDA, Joint Agricultural Weather Facility, USDA South Building, Room 5844, Washington, DC 20250.

MICHIGAN CLIMATE INFORMATION

If you want more detailed information about the places listed in the "Michigan Local Climate Data" section of this book, or want some pamphlets, maps, or specific facts about Michigan's climate, call or write your State Climatologist, MDA/Climatology Program, 417 Natural Science Building, Michigan State University, East Lansing, MI 48824 (phone 517-355-0231). If you have a computer with a modem, ask about their menu-driven Climate Bulletin Board.

GREAT LAKES

Michigan residents can get—free of charge—a nifty series of brochures about the Great Lakes (one for each lake, and one about the Great Lakes in general) by writing the Michigan Sea Grant College Program at the University of Michigan, 2200 Bonisteel Blvd., Ann Arbor, MI 48109, or at Michigan State University, 334 Natural Resources Bldg., East Lansing, MI 48824-1222. The six brochures are 25¢ each for nonresidents.

The Great Lakes Environmental Research Laboratory, 2205 Commonwealth Blvd., Ann Arbor, MI 48105-1593, publishes technical and some not-so-technical literature about the lakes; write their Publications Office for a list.

For detailed information on the ever-changing fluctuations of the lakes, write the Department of the Army, Detroit District Corps of Engineers, Attn: CENCE-ED-L, P.O. Box 1027, Detroit, MI 48231 for a free copy of the latest "Monthly Bulletin of Lake Levels for the Great Lakes."

AUDIOVISUALS

Films, videos, and slide sets about various aspects of the weather abound, if you know where to look. Edward A. Brotak, Atmospheric Sciences Program, UNC Asheville, NC 28804 has put together a long list of audiovisuals that you can buy or rent. The list costs two dollars.

The National Weather Service has a wide selection of pamphlets, slide sets, and films available to schools, groups and individuals for purchase or loan. Their catalog of Weather and Flood Hazard Awareness Material can be obtained from: National Weather Service, Disaster Preparedness Staff W/OM11x1, Silver Spring Metro Center II, East-West Highway, Silver Spring, MD 20910, or from your local NWS office.

The Aurora Color Television Project, Geophysical Institute, University of Alaska, Fairbanks, AK 99775-0800, has a wonderful 24-minute video of the aurora borealis at its best (set to classical music!) It costs about $1.50 a minute, but if you like the northern lights, it's worth it.

DAILY WEATHER INFORMATION

Weather will never really make much sense unless you follow it each and every day. You don't have to take your own records; there's plenty of data available in the media and elsewhere. Along with the daily high and low temperatures across the country, most newspapers carry weather maps, satellite photos, and lists of daily high and low temperatures. However, newspaper maps aren't very informative. For a good, detailed weather map, I recommend the daily surface and upper-air maps published in weekly booklets by the Climate Analysis Center, Room 808, World Weather Building, Washington, DC 20233, for $60 a year. One of my prize possessions is a 40-year collection of these maps!

Television weather broadcasts vary in quality; some of the better ones are actually quite informative. Most show time-lapse satellite photographs of moving storms and clouds—a perspective on the workings of the weather that didn't exist just 20 years ago! Watch them for a while and you'll get a real feel for how storms grow, move, and die. Probably the most complete broadcast television weather report is "A.M. Weather." Produced in cooperation with the National Weather Service, this 15-minute report airs weekday mornings on most Public TV stations. Write to A.M. Weather, Owings Mill, MD 21117 for a brochure and station listing.

On cable television, "The Weather Channel" gives comprehensive, continuous, and current weather reports.

WEATHER ON THE RADIO

The weather is a subject of passing fancy to some and passionate interest to others. However, for many people—notably mariners, aviators, and truckers—the whims of the winds are matters of economic welfare and even personal safety. To fill the needs of these people, an amazing variety of weather information is broadcast over a variety of radio frequencies. The airwaves are free, and you're all welcome to listen to these broadcasts—all you need is the proper radio for the frequency band of the broadcast.

Speaking of frequencies, those listed below are in kilohertz (kHz) and Megahertz (MHz), formerly known as kilocycles and megacycles. One megahertz equals 1,000 kilohertz, so, for example, the standard AM broadcast band extends from 530 to 1600 kHz, or 0.53 to 1.6 MHz. Here's a sampler of what's available:

AM Radio. Of course, you can hear your local weather forecast on an ordinary AM radio. (By the way, AM stands for amplitude modulation, which describes the way the voice and music information is carried by the radio waves.) At night, when the electrons in the high atmosphere settle down and form a sort of a mirror to radio waves, you can pick up AM stations hundreds of miles away.

It's fun to listen to what the weather is like in remote places such as St. Louis (1120 kHz), Denver (850 kHz) and Winnipeg (580 kHz), and the information can be useful in making your own local forecasts. I recall some dramatic live descriptions of the eye of Hurricane Betsy when it passed over New Orleans (870 kHz) in 1965.

Some stations, like Fort Worth (820 kHz), broadcast detailed national "Weather Along the highways" reports to motorists and truckers.

Weather Radio. For up-to-date local weather information, your best bet by far is your nearest National Weather Service "Weather Radio" station. The continuous broadcasts give forecasts, warnings, and observations for the area covered by the 25- to 50-mile range of the stations. There are hundreds of these stations in the U.S.A. and dozens in Canada; from Michigan you can tune in broadcasts from Alpena, Detroit, Flint, Grand Rapids, Houghton, Marquette, Onondaga (near Lansing), Sault Ste. Marie, and Traverse City, as well as from Toledo (OH), South Bend (IN), Green Bay and Park Falls (WI), and Windsor and Sault Ste. Marie (Ontario). The National Weather Service, Attn: W/OM15x2, NOAA, Silver Spring, MD 20910 has a free brochure and station list describing the service. You can listen to these weather broadcasts on "police band" radios and scanners on 162.40, 162.475, or 162.55 MHz and on special "weather radios" designed solely for these broadcasts. Some weather radios sound an alarm or switch on automatically whenever the local station broadcasts a severe weather warning! Several models in the $20 to $50 range are available from Maxon (8610

NW 107th Terrace, Kansas City, MO 64153; these are sold in electronics, hardware and department stores) and from Radio Shack.

Aviation and Marine Radio. Those who live near airports or Great Lake ports will find more sources of weather information in the "very high frequency" (VHF) marine (156-162 MHz) and aviation (108-136 MHz) bands. Some broadcast continuous weather reports, while others send out warnings and answer requests for specific information. One particularly interesting aviation frequency is 122 MHz, where pilots report their airborne weather observations to the ground. You can buy special marine and aviation radios to receive these transmissions, or listen on the VHF bands of multi-band radios and scanners (make sure the radio includes the aviation band).

Excellent guides to marine weather broadcasts are the "Marine Weather Services Charts" that show, in map format, weather broadcast stations for the Great Lakes and 14 other coastal regions of the United States, including Alaska, Hawaii, and Puerto Rico. Chart MSC-11 covers Lakes Superior and Michigan, while Chart MSC-12 spans Lakes Huron, Erie, and Ontario. They're $1.25 each from the National Ocean Service, Distribution Branch N/CG33, Riverdale MD 20737-1199, or from marine supply shops.

Canadian broadcast schedules appear in "Radio Aids to Marine Navigation," available from the Canadian Government Publishing Center, Ottawa K1A 0S9.

Ham Radio. When severe weather threatens, the National Weather Service relies on volunteer spotters to call in sightings of hail, funnel clouds, and such. Many of these spotters are amateur radio operators (or "hams") out in their cars with their mobile radio rigs. If you want to listen to these live reports, tune your radio or scanner to the 144-148 MHz band (specific frequencies are listed in the "ARRL Net Directory"—for $1—from the American Radio Relay League, Newington, CT 06111); if you would rather be out there yourself watching and reporting the weather, ask your local Weather Service or Civil Defense office about joining the "Skywarn" program.

Shortwave Radio. To hear some truly exotic weather reports, get a shortwave radio. The so-called shortwave band, 2 to 30 MHz (or 2,000 to 30,000 kHz), is unique in the radio spectrum in that its signals can travel literally around the world. They do this by reflecting off ionospheric layers, like AM radio waves, but since the higher frequencies of shortwave signals bounce off higher layers of the ionosphere, they travel farther. I've been able to pick up weather reports from Africa, Australia, and Siberia! As you toast your toes by the fireplace on a subzero night, you can listen to hurricane advisories from Fiji.

Here are some frequencies of interest to Michiganders—keep in mind that frequencies less than 10,000 kHz (10 MHz) are generally received better at night, and higher frequencies are stronger during the day.

2514, 4369, 4381, and 8794 kHz—Station WLC in Rogers City, MI, broadcasts Great Lakes weather forecasts and warnings, along with shipboard weather reports, several times a day. The "Marine Weather Services Charts" mentioned above describes the content of these broadcasts in detail. Schedules are subject to change, but try 2:45 A.M., 4:45 A.M., 8:45 A.M., and 10:45 A.M., and 2:45 P.M., 4:45 P.M., 8:45 P.M., and 10:45 P.M. Eastern Time.

3485, 6604, 10051, and 13270 kHz—Continuous airport weather reports from the eastern parts of the U.S. and Canada, transmitted from New York and Gander, Newfoundland. At approximately 1 and 31 minutes past each hour you'll hear the latest weather report from Detroit Metro Airport. These broadcasts are aimed at transatlantic airliners and can usually be heard in Europe, so next time you're visiting Finland you can listen to the weather back home!

6753 and 15035 kHz—Canadian and Arctic weather reports broadcast from Edmonton, Alberta; Trenton, Ontario; and St. John's, Newfoundland, at 20, 30 and 40 minutes (respectively) past each hour. When Edmonton reports temperatures below -30° (Celsius, eh!), watch out—a cold wave may be on its way.

6673, 8893, 10015, 11246, 13244, 13267, and 13354 kHz—Just some of the frequencies used by Air Force and NOAA "Hurricane Hunter" flights. You might even hear a report from the eye of a hurricane!

2500, 5000, 10000, 15000, and 20000 kHz—The nation's official time station, WWV in Fort Collins, CO, broadcasts beeps every second (exactly!) 24 hours a day, along with storm warnings for the Atlantic, Caribbean, Gulf of Mexico, and North Pacific, beginning at 8 minutes past each hour. On good days you might hear storm warnings for the South Pacific from WWVH (Hawaii), on the same frequencies (except 20000 kHz), at 48 minutes past the hour. WWV also broadcasts solar activity reports at 18 minutes past the hour. If the report predicts a "major" or "severe" geomagnetic storm, keep your eyes on the sky—there may be some northern lights. You can hear the same solar report by dialing 303-497-3235.

Most general stores don't carry shortwave radios, so you'll have to shop around. One of the best readily available radios is the Radio Shack DX-390. For a wider selection, check the specialty shops like Electronic Equipment Bank (137 Church St. N.W., Vienna, VA 22180), Universal Radio (1280 Aida Drive, Reynoldsburg, OH 43068), or Grove Enterprises (P.O. Box 98, Brasstown, NC 28902), or peruse the ads in one of the monthly radio magazines, like *Monitoring Times* (same address as Grove Enterprises) or Popular Communications (76 North Broadway, Hicksville, NY 11801).

A suitable radio will cost at least $150; if you want to spend less, try your luck at a local Amateur Radio Club swap meet (or "Hamfest"). Just be sure the thing works before you pay for it!

Except for the time signal station WWV, all of these weather broadcasts are in Single Side Band (SSB) mode, so get a radio with a SSB switch or a Beat Frequency Oscillator (BFO) dial. Also make sure the radio tunes to the frequency bands you want. Finally, don't forget the antenna—for less than $10, you can string up a 50-foot wire that will work wonders.

Weather Fax. With a good shortwave radio, a computer, and a "demodulator" connecting the two, you can receive facsimile weather maps broadcast by the U.S. Air Force and the U.S. and Canadian Coast Guards. Starting from scratch, the entire setup could cost $1,000 or more, but it's a lot less if you already have the radio and computer. The least expensive demodulator I know of is made by Software Systems Consulting, 615 S. El Camino Real, San Clemente, CA 92672, for about $99. You can also subscribe to over-the-wire fax services; check the ads in the *Bulletin of the American Meteorological Society* or *Weatherwise*.

Weather Satellites. You can skip the middleman and get satellite photos straight from the source by tuning in satellites as they pass overhead. All you need is a good radio tuned to the proper VHF or UHF (Ultra-High Frequency) frequencies, a computer, and the appropriate software. For some satellites you don't even need a special antenna. Once more, look in the radio magazines for details.

Thunder and Lightning. Yes, the weather itself broadcasts on a wide range of radio frequencies. You have doubtless heard the annoying static from nearby thunderstorms on your AM radio—that's because your cheap little radio is actually a pretty good lightning detector. Just tune the radio between stations, and you'll hear every lightning strike within 50 miles (farther at night). After a bit of practice, you'll be able to gauge the distance and intensity of the storm by noting how loud and frequent the static crashes are. If your radio has a signal strength meter, or "Vu-meter," the meter reading of the static will go up as the storm gets closer. Another trick is to rotate the radio until the static level drops off or disappears. At that point, the antenna (usually a black rod with copper wire coiled around it, running lengthwise inside the case) points directly at the storm. You may have to guess which end of the antenna is pointed toward the storm, though. Years ago the Forest Service used direction-finding radios to locate lightning storms for fire fighting purposes. Now, you can use your radio to wisely decide when to shut off your computer or get out of (or off of) the water.

WEATHER ON YOUR COMPUTER

Computers are getting their little chips into everything, including weather. There's a rapidly growing number of weather-related products and services that can turn your computer into a weather information station. Among the available products are:

Software (programs) for forecasting weather, keeping records, charting storm tracks, and graphing weather data.

Data sets, on disk, of all sorts of climate records. A single floppy disk can hold decades of daily temperatures and rainfall for your favorite weather station, and a single optical disk—the computer equivalent of a musical compact disk—can contain decades of daily climate data for thousands of weather stations. For more about this, write: National Climatic Data Center, Federal Building, Asheville, NC 28801-2696, or EarthInfo, Inc., 5541 Central Ave., Boulder, CO 80301-2846.

Bulletin board services you can dial up (if you have a modem to connect your computer to the telephone) for national and global weather data and forecasts. Some bulletin boards allow you to receive weather maps and satellite photos on your computer, and there are similar services that will print the maps on a facsimile machine. The Michigan State Climatologist (MDA/Climatology Program, 417 Natural Science Building, Michigan State University, East Lansing, MI 48824) has a bulletin board on which you can find out how much snow fell at Bad Axe in 1939, among other things.

New computer products appear nearly every day, so keep checking the ads in the *Bulletin of the American Meteorological Society, the American Weather Observer*, or *Weatherwise*.

WEATHER INSTRUMENTS

Of course, you want to set up a weather station in your back yard. Whether you go for the basics—a home-made, tin-can rain gauge and a household thermometer—or a fancy computerized set-up that even records the amount of ozone in the air depends on the depth of your interest and of your wallet. Some of the more common instruments, like thermometers, barometers, and rain gauges, are carried by department and hardware stores. Radio Shack carries several relatively inexpensive electronic weather instruments. For a wider selection, try the catalogs available from:

American Weather Enterprises, P.O. Box 1383, Media, PA 19063

Edmund Scientific, 101 E. Gloucester Pike, Barrington, NJ 08007

Robert E White Instruments, 34 Commercial Wharf, Boston, MA 02110

Science Associates, 31 Airpark Road, Box 230, Princeton, NJ 08542

Weathertrac, P.O. Box 122, Cedar Falls, IA 50613

Weatherwise Books and Instruments, Main St., New London, NH 03527

Wind & Weather, P.O. Box 2320, Mendocino, CA 95460.

More specifically, the best rain gauges for their prices are the plastic "wedge" made by Tru-Chek, Albert Lea, MN 56007, for under $10, and the $26.95 gauge sold by the American Weather Observer, 401 Whitney Blvd., Belvidere, IL 61008. Most commercial lightning detectors are dreadfully expensive, but you can buy one that picks up lightning 50 miles away for under $50 from McCallie Manufacturing Corp., P.O. Box 77, Brownsboro, AL 35741.

One dandy little weather instrument that money can't buy is a thing called a "hail pad." Hail is as infrequent as it is important, and it's easy to miss a hail event by simply being away at work, in the basement, or asleep when it happens. The solution is a hail pad, which is nothing more than a slab of beaded styrofoam (like the stuff cheap picnic coolers are made of) wrapped in heavy-duty aluminum foil. Set it outside, weigh down the edges with bricks to keep it from blowing away, and when hail strikes, the cratered surface of the pad vividly records the storm. This dirt-cheap device was perfected by researchers in Illinois, who found it more reliable than high-tech gizmos with lasers and sound recorders. If your hail measures three-quarters of an inch or more in diameter, call the Weather Service immediately—stones that large are considered "severe weather" and potentially damaging, and forecasters want to know about it. If you find a hailstone 17 inches or more in circumference, put it in your freezer and protect it with your life—you may have the Hope Diamond of meteorology!

ASK THE EXPERTS

Sometimes you can get literature about the weather from various outfits that deal with the subject. Among these are the Meteorology, Agriculture, and Geography departments at colleges and universities and your local Weather Service. Michigan has National Weather Service Offices in Alpena, Ann Arbor, Detroit, Flint, Grand Rapids, Houghton Lake, Lansing, Marquette, Muskegon, and Sault Ste. Marie. (Try not to call when the weather is acting up—they'll probably be quite busy.) Some local TV stations have pamphlets about weather. The

National Center for Atmospheric Research, P.O. Box 3000, Boulder, Colorado 80303, is in the forefront of weather research, and their Information Office has some interesting public relations blurbs.

CLUBS & SOCIETIES

Meteorologists like to whoop it up just like everyone else, and have their own groups for doing so. I've already mentioned the American Meteorological Society, 45 Beacon Street, Boston, MA 02108, which appeals mostly to professionals. However, there's a Southeast Michigan Chapter that welcomes the public at meetings; it's a good place to meet some meteorologists and enjoy interesting presentations. For details, write to the A.M.S. in Boston or contact the local chapter's officers (as of 1992): Paul Gross at WDIV-TV in Detroit and James Geyer at WLNS-TV in Lansing.

WDIV (622 W. Lafayette Blvd., Detroit, MI 48321) also has a "Weather Watchers" group you might want to check out. And yes, there *really* is a Green Flash Society! They're headquartered at Tiffany's Ice Cream Parlour in Empire (P.O. Box 297, Empire, MI 49630).

ASTRONOMY

Many meteorologists also have an interest in that bit of the universe that lies above the clouds. For more information on watching the night sky, I recommend picking up one of the astro-magazines: *Astronomy* (P.O. Box 1612, Waukesha, WI 53187; phone 800-446-5489) or *Sky & Telescope* (49 Bay State Road, Cambridge, MA 02138; phone 800-253-6117). The Abrams Planetarium (Michigan State University, East Lansing, MI 48824) publishes a monthly *Sky Calendar* for $6 a year, and has a telephone "Starline" (517-332-STAR) that announces events in the sky. Other planetariums are located in Alpena, Ann Arbor, Battle Creek, Bloomfield Hills, Detroit, Flint, Grand Rapids, Kalamazoo, Lansing, and Marquette.

There are also 19 local astronomy clubs in Michigan. A complete list of astronomy clubs, planetariums, computer bulletin boards, and telescope dealers appears each year in the September issue of *Sky & Telescope* (or separately for $1).

And, if it bothers you that you can't see the Milky Way from your backyard on a clear night because we're sending millions of dollars of electric lighting into outer space every year, the International Dark-Sky Association (3545 N. Stewart Ave., Tucson, AZ 85716) has literature about nighttime light pollution and what you can do about it.

VOLCANOES

It may be stretching it a bit to include volcanoes in a book about weather, but since major volcanic eruptions could affect the climate, some of you might want to keep tabs on them. The monthly *Bulletin of the Global Volcanism Network* gives details of all volcanic events—major, minor, and suspected—around the world. The *Bulletin* is $18 per year from: American Geophysical Union, 2000 Florida Avenue NW, Washington, DC 20009; phone 800-966-2481.

LAST, BUT NOT LEAST

Reading *Michigan Weather*, and every other weather book, from cover to cover, subscribing to all the weather magazines and climate reports, buying a barometer and a weather radio, and joining all the meteorological societies will not make you—or anyone— an expert on the weather. As Yogi Berra said, "You can observe a lot by just watching," and the way to become a weather expert is to watch it—frequently! So don't forget to look out your window once in a while. Take note of the changing clouds, the ups and downs of the thermometer, and (when it's clear) the northern lights. Put your boots on and stick a ruler in the snow. And be sure to write down your observations so you can read them years later. You'll find patterns to your local weather that no one could have ever told you about, and you'll find the total disregard the weather can often have for those patterns. After ten or twenty years you might have some idea of what people mean by "climate change." Above all, you'll begin to understand and appreciate the weather like an old friend—a friend who is always there!

INDEX

■■■■■■■■■■■■■■■■■■■■■■■■■■

Richard A. Keen received a doctorate in climatology from the University of Colorado in 1979, and is self-employed as a writer/photographer specializing in weather. He has worked as a tornado spotter and forecaster, a storm meteorologist and a shortwave radio monitor, and is the author of *Skywatch: The Western Weather Guide* and *Skywatch: The Eastern Weather Guide*, both published by Fulcrum Press, and *Minnesota Weather*, published by American & World Geographic Publishing.